Quality Service: The Restaurant Manager's Bible

Cornell University
School of Hotel Administration

Quality Service: The Restaurant Manager's Bible

Printed in the United States of America by Brodock Press
Photocomposition by Partners Composition
ISBN 0-937056-05-7

Quality Service:

The Restaurant Manager's Bible

Andy!

Read & enjoy

Conviviality every time you go out to eat — Don't ya? Bill

To Gary, Dick, and Cliff,

without whose introduction to the essence of service,
this book would not have been possible.

Contents

AS A consultant specializing in training and development for a variety of food-service organizations and as a food-service consumer, I have found that service is the weak link in far too many restaurants. Owners, operators, and managers talk a lot about service (and may try to train their employees for it), but they tend to put the bulk of their energies into other areas of the operation. The result is that customers keep complaining about the service they receive. In fact, the single biggest gripe of American restaurant customers, year after year, is *service*.

With this in mind, I started researching three basic questions: What constitutes "quality" service? Why is good service found in some operations and not in others? And what can restaurant operators do to improve their service?

Obviously, the main factor in achieving service quality is *people,* and that is what this book is all about; how people act, react, and interact in restaurants—whether quick-service, self-service, or full-service.

Two groups of people are essential to the food-service transaction. The first group is food-service personnel—food servers, beverage servers, counter persons, window persons, supervisors, and managers. The second group comprises the people without whom there

Preface

would be no business at all—the customers. This book is about how food-service personnel can learn to interact more successfully with the customers to ensure that the customers get the service they want.

This volume was written for restaurant owners, operators, managers, and students. While it is not intended to be a training manual for food and beverage servers, it contains a practical, easy-to-read explanation of the nature of service in food-service operations, and it describes how quality service can be made a reality. I have tried to provide a complete analysis of all the components of quality service, and what you—as an owner, operator, or manager—must do to assemble these components. I hope this book will help expand the small but growing cadre of enlightened restaurateurs, managers, and service personnel who are truly attuned to the "people side" of the enterprise.

William B. Martin
Claremont, California

May 1986

Peas, Potatoes, and People

1

MOST OF us in the food-service business understand and appreciate the fact that restaurants are a unique form of enterprise.

Restaurants not only produce a product and sell it, but they also handle the distribution and facilitate the consumption of the product. In most food-service establishments, all these processes are orchestrated under one roof, within one operation.

Yet few of us in the restaurant business fully understand and appreciate the fact that outside the site of production—the kitchen—the operation's complexity multiplies geometrically. Furthermore, few of us realize that outside of the kitchen "people skills" become more critical to the success of the operation than technical skills.

If we fail to understand the complexity of the people side of the business, we are in trouble. And, in fact, many of us take it for granted. We get stuck in the "peas and potatoes" side of the enterprise and hope that the people side will somehow take care of itself.

This assumption is unfortunate, because people skills are far more complex than technical skills. When service personnel begin to interact with customers, human behavior takes on great importance to the operation's success. Because of its complexity, human behavior must not be left to chance in a restaurant. Whenever human behavior is involved, we must consider the psychological, sociological, and anthropological world of human emotions, needs, wants, expectations, rules, cognition, and ways of communicating, and we must deal with behavior modifiers, behavior reinforcers, and behavior "extinguishers," *ad infinitum.*

In short, we cannot concentrate exclusively on the technical side of the enterprise. We must deal with the people side, for when we leave the kitchen, we enter the complex theater of human behavior commonly referred to as service.

Service as an Endangered Activity

Service: we praise it or curse it, seek it or avoid it, but most of the time we do little to change it. But change it we must, because year after year consumers cite service as the greatest irritant in restaurants. In fact, for four years in a row, more than 70 percent of restaurant patrons have stated that service was a problem in the restaurants they visited.[1] We know service is important, and we know it would be difficult (if not impossible) to run a food-service operation without it, but so far service has been a stumbling block to restaurant customers' satisfaction.

A former president of the National Restaurant Association, Thad Eure, has asked the question: "If we're doing so well, why are we under attack?" He saw that the major problem within the restaurant industry is not one of delivering food or providing perceived value to the customer. Instead, he said, the industry's major problem is its inability to provide personal service. He said, pointedly, "We need to strengthen our bond with the customer . . . our real problems are people problems."[2]

Eure's assessment is on target. Quality service is the exception rather than the rule in too many food-service operations. In establishments that are providing deficient service, the personnel simply don't know how to treat customers, and customers are actually being victimized. I believe the owners and operators of these restaurants have an incomplete understanding of the total nature of service; they fail to apply the same clear expectations to service that they use to evaluate the quality and value of their food. Since they haven't stopped to think specifically about the service that should character-

---

[1]"Tastes of America," *Restaurants & Institutions,* December 1980, 1981, 1982, 1983; December 5, 1984, p. 102. The 1985 results were based on 1,381 mail-survey returns from households across the U.S.

[2]Thad Eure, "NRA: If We're Doing So Well, Why Are We Under Attack?," *Food Service Marketing,* January 1979, p. 53.

ize their restaurant, they unknowingly reward and reinforce inappropriate or impersonal behavior in their service personnel.

Many service personnel *do* know how to treat customers, and many others *think* they do. Yet employees all too often fail to make customer relations a priority in performing their jobs. They mistakenly believe quality service involves only timeliness. This factor is certainly important, but there is much more to quality service than getting the product out on time. Our fast-paced American lifestyle places so much emphasis on speed and efficiency that it is easy to forget how important it is for customers to be treated thoughtfully, considerately, and attentively by those who serve them. Being prompt isn't necessarily the same as being nice. In fact, the most expeditious food servers can be the least personal and friendly.

The more this limited view of quality service is perpetuated, the more the people side of service tends to be either neglected or abandoned altogether. Quality service demands more than promptness and efficiency. It demands that customers be treated with respect, kindness, and consideration. This is what the people side of service is all about.

As this book will show, owners, operators, and food-service personnel can develop a holistic view of quality service and come to appreciate how customers should be treated. We can come to understand the importance of people as well as peas and potatoes. By using the right actions and reinforcement, restaurant operators can significantly improve the people skills of their service personnel. We can provide effective feedback and rewards that modify behavior. In turn, restaurant consumers will get the kind of service they want and expect—*quality service*. This book will help you accomplish just that.

Improving Customer Service: A Five-Step Process

Improving service in restaurants requires changing people's behavior. Before we can affect the level of service, we must change the behavior of managers, service personnel, and maybe even customers. Changing behavior means altering what people do and how they do it, what they say and how they say it.

Certainly we must also deal with knowledge and attitudes. And the strategies explained in this book address ways to change the knowledge and attitudes of managers, service personnel, and customers. But if the steps we take to improve customer service end with knowledge and attitudes, we will make little headway. *Behavioral* change is what we're after—nothing less.

Five major steps are required to change behavior and generate quality service (See Figure 1-1):

(1) Clear and concise descriptions of the *desired behavior* must be established. A clear idea of what is expected must precede any formal plan to improve service behavior.
(2) Your current service *strengths and weaknesses* must be assessed so that improvement strategies concentrate on those areas where service is deficient, while areas of strength can be supported and reinforced.
(3) A workable *strategy for training* must be generated. To be effective, training must have purpose and direction, which clear expectations can provide.
(4) The *implementation* of strategies to improve customer service must be designed to suit your operation and be incremental in approach.
(5) The behavior that produces quality service must be encouraged with *feedback,* positive consequences, and rewards. Any change in behavior brought about by effective training will soon fade without careful implementation of your service-improvement plans, followed by effective inducements that reinforce the desired behavior.

If you ignore these five steps or take shortcuts, you will gain little ground in improving your operation's service. The five steps constitute a complete process for improving service in your operation by nurturing the behavioral changes you desire. The chapters of this book follow the five-step process. Chapter 2 shows the customer's perspective on service. Chapter 3 explains the unique role of service in a dining experience. Chapters 4 and 5 provide a detailed analysis of the essence of service from two complementary standpoints— "procedural" and "convivial." Chapter 6 will help you define specifically what quality service means for your operation.

Figure 1-1

The Five-Step Process for Improving Customer Service

I.

Define Your Standards of Quality Service with Measurable Indicators

II.

Assess Your Current Situation

III.

Develop Effective Service-Improvement Strategies

IV.

Initiate Your Solutions Carefully

V.

Provide Feedback, Recognition, and Rewards

Chapter 7 describes how to use two specific tools—the "Customer-Service Audit" and the "Customer-Service Assessment Scale"—to measure and evaluate your current customer-service strengths and weaknesses. Chapter 8 focuses on the characteristics of effective service-improvement strategies and outlines a number of specific training strategies that can improve customer service. Chapter 9 provides suggestions for planning and implementing service-improvement strategies that will greatly increase your chances of success. Finally, Chapter 10 suggests ways to provide the all-important feedback to service personnel, as well as how to reinforce the behavior that you desire from your service staff.

These five steps to improving customer service should be considered five integrated components of a single effort. Each is simple and direct, but none can stand alone; each step serves to reinforce and complement the others. Together these five steps will greatly enhance the level of service your customers receive.

The Case of John and Carol Pleasant

2

TO UNDERSTAND what service is all about, it is helpful to look at it first through the eyes of your customers. You need to see what they see and experience what they experience. Identifying with the customer is the crucial first step in augmenting the quality of service in any food-service operation.

The case of "John and Carol Pleasant" illustrates a dining experience typical of many restaurants. Although the example is of a table-service restaurant, the story could have taken place at any kind of operation. Regardless of your restaurant type, the case of the Pleasants has implications for all food-service operators. This case provides insight into how service is separate and unique from the meal itself and other factors that constitute a total dining experience. With this in mind, let's meet John and Carol Pleasant, archetypal diners.

John and Carol probably dine out about as often as any other couple with an active family. They like to reward themselves occasionally by going out for an evening without the children. Caught up in their busy suburban lifestyle, John and Carol have come to rely on their "nights of escape" as a necessary part of their lives. They look forward to these times together. Both enjoy a nice quiet evening out— just the two of them, with no noise or annoyances, and no cooking or dishes.

Having lived in their community for more than five years, the Pleasants have developed some old standbys, but they have never really developed a firm loyalty to any one restaurant. In fact, they *enjoy* trying different restaurants. Carol likes the adventure, and John likes the diversity. Living in a large metropolitan area, the Pleasants have many dining-out alternatives. Most of the dinnerhouse chains operate restaurants within a comfortable driving distance. With these and the plethora of fast-food and independent family restaurants, the Pleasants have never felt a lack of restaurants from which to choose. If anything, they often feel overwhelmed by the vast assortment of choices available to them.

After discussing several alternatives for their Saturday escape, John and Carol decide to try a relatively new dinnerhouse that their neighbors have recommended. Carol's neighbor frequently raves about the food at the Run o' the Mill restaurant. John always enjoys the chance to get a steak dinner, while Carol hopes to find Alaskan king crab on the menu.

It is Saturday night. The children are attended to, and John and Carol are off. Pulling away from the house they both breathe a small sigh of relief. "You know, John," Carol confides, "I really do enjoy the children, but it sure is nice to get away like this. We really should do this more often." John nods in agreement.

Half-way there, John asks, "By the way, do we have reservations at this place?"

"No. I called, but they don't take them."

The Run o' the Mill is a freestanding restaurant situated adjacent to a regional shopping mall.

It is close to seven o'clock when the Pleasants pull into its parking lot. Both are ready for a relaxing evening.

"Look at all the cars!," Carol exclaims. "I hope we don't have a long wait."

As Carol and John walk up to the front door, they notice the striking facade of the building. Its unusual juxtaposition of wood and brick is accentuated by numerous floodlights placed in strategic locations around the building.

"Someone has spent a bundle on this place," John comments.

"It's gorgeous, isn't it?," Carol responds.

As they enter, Carol notices that the wood-and-brick theme of the exterior is carried through to the interior. Terra-cotta floors are beautifully accented by a butcher block atop the front desk.

At first glance, the Pleasants can't tell whether there is a wait or not. The cocktail lounge looks full. John sneaks a peek into the dining room. It also looks full, not altogether a bad sign. "Something must be going right here," he thinks to himself.

A youthful hostess, dressed conservatively in a tailored skirt and blouse, is standing behind the front desk. She appears to be counting something.

As the Pleasants approach, she looks up and says, "Oh. Just one minute. I'll be right with you." John and Carol look at each other, smile uneasily and quietly wait. After a rather long minute the hostess looks up again and says, "We're running about a half-hour wait. Shall I put you on the list?"

"Boy, she doesn't mess around," John thinks. Aloud, he says, "Sure, we'll wait."

"Name?," the hostess asks, without looking up. John dutifully recites and spells their name.

"Okay. I'll call you when your table is ready," the hostess informs them, as she continues her counting.

Abruptly left to fend for themselves, John and Carol decide they might as well wait in the lounge. Carol locates a vacant table for two back in a corner. After they sit down, they spot only one cocktail waitress, who is at the other side of the lounge busily delivering drinks to waiting customers. Since the one waitress is busy, Carol decides it might be a good time to suggest some redecorating ideas she has come up with for the living room. John, however, seems to be preoccupied.

"What are you frowning about, dear?," Carol asks.

"Oh, I was just thinking about that hostess."

"She was cute, but a little young for you, don't you think?," Carol says with a smile.

"I wasn't thinking about her looks. She just wasn't nice at all, was she?"

"Well," Carol responds, "She's probably new. We're here to relax. Let's not let an 18-year-old hostess, of all things, get the better of us."

"You're right," John concedes. "But I wonder where that cocktail waitress went."

While they wait, Carol attacks at length the dated drapes, the threadbare sofa, and the lack of a conversation area in their living room.

"I wonder where that cocktail waitress is?" is John's only response.

Ten minutes later a different waitress appears. She seems to be nervous and somewhat harried. "Boy, this place is a real zoo tonight," she says in greeting. "I'm supposed to be in the dining room, not the bar, but they're getting blown out in here. What can I get you?"

After that introduction, John thinks he should make it as easy as possible for the waitress. "Two glasses of white wine, please."

She nods and sprints away as fast as she appeared.

Neither John nor Carol is a wine connoisseur. Carol couldn't care less. She just enjoys a nice glass of white wine from time to time. But John feels somewhat insecure about his lack of wine knowledge. He usually makes it a practice to ask the server what label of wine the restaurant serves. Over the years he has developed some favorites, and other wines he tries to avoid. He now realizes he has forgotten to ask the waitress the name of the house wine. "I'll ask her when she comes back," he tells himself.

Carol is still eager to talk about the living room. As usual with discussions about the house, she does most of the talking and John does most of the listening and nodding. After a considerable length of time, they have yet to receive their wine.

"How long have we been waiting for our wine?," John asks.

"Only a few minutes, honey. Relax."

John can't help but look around for the waitress. He finally locates her carrying a full tray of drinks. Two glasses of white wine appear to be part of her load. As the waitress works her way through the lounge, John can't help feel some empathy for her. "Probably overworked and underpaid," he comments to Carol.

The waitress finally arrives at the Pleasants' table. "Boy, are we busy tonight," she says without a smile as she places the full wine glasses down. "And my feet are killing me. Sorry it took me so long. We have a rookie bartender tonight, of all nights. That will be three dollars, please."

"We plan to have dinner here. Can you put this on our dinner tab?," John asks.

"Sorry, can't do that," the waitress answers abruptly. Without further argument, John reaches into his wallet and hands the waitress a five-dollar bill. While balancing her tray with one hand, she makes change with the other. She strategically leaves a dollar and four quarters in change on a little black tray and is gone like the breeze.

"Shoot, I was going to ask her what kind of wine this is," John laments.

"It's *good* wine," Carol responds with her usual good humor. "Try it."

Sometime later John notes the time. "How long have we been waiting, anyway?," he asks.

At that very moment, the Pleasants hear over the paging system, "Pleasant party of two, your table is ready. Pleasant party of two."

John and Carol have long since finished their glasses of wine, and since the cocktail waitress never returned to offer refills, the dollar and four quarters are still sitting where she left them. John picks up the dollar and two of the quarters and leaves the remaining two quarters for the waitress.

As the Pleasants enter the lobby, John notices that the hostess who greeted them still has her nose directed toward the stack of papers on the desk. Another young, nice-looking girl asks, "Are you the Pleasant party?"

John and Carol nod in unison.

"This way," the girl commands and takes off as if someone had fired a starting pistol for the hundred-meter dash. After a moment, John locates the fleet-footed hostess waiting for them on the other side of the dining room, and he guides Carol in that direction.

As John and Carol sit down, the hostess hands them each a menu and says, "This is your menu. Your waiter this evening will be Gary." With that, she is off as quickly as she arrived.

John glances briefly at the menu and notes that the restaurant has the steak he likes to order. While Carol studies the menu at length, John glances around the dining room. The decor and design seem tastefully done, although somewhat eclectic. The wood-and-brick theme is carried throughout, set off by brass fixtures and railings and a variety of potted plants everywhere.

"What are you going to have?," Carol asks.

"The New York strip."

"I should have known. I was all set for the Alaskan king crab, but they have some other seafood dinners that look scrumptious. I can't decide."

"Why don't you ask Gary for help?"

"Gary?"

"He's supposed to be our waiter, but I haven't seen him anywhere."

Time passes. Finally Gary approaches the table. "Can I get you anything from the bar?," he asks, sounding as though his speech were preprogrammed.

John looks at Carol, and Carol looks at John. John decides, "No, I guess not. We've just come from the lounge. But we would like to order some wine with dinner."

"Oh, I see you don't have a wine list. Let me go get you one," Gary says and is off. While they wait, John remembers he wants to ask about the house wine.

Gary bounds back with the wine list in hand. He gives it to John.

"What's your house wine?," John asks. "We had some in the lounge and enjoyed it."

"Bottle Brothers," the waiter responds. "Not too 'chablis,' is it?"

Ignoring Gary's pun, Carol responds, "Oh, I really like it. John, why don't we just get more of the same?"

"Well, in that case, you won't be needing this," Gary says, sounding somewhat annoyed. He reaches for the wine list, but John holds onto it. He cajoles, "Come on, Carol! We owe ourselves a nice bottle of wine. Don't you think so?"

"I'm easy," Carol says with a smile.

Feeling somewhat insecure about his ability to pick a decent wine, John asks the waiter for his advice.

"Well," the waiter replies, "all the wines on our list are very good."

"That helps a lot!," John thinks to himself. But he says, "Well, how about the white wines? Which one would you recommend?"

"To tell you the truth, I'm not much of a wine drinker. I really don't know what to tell you," Gary says.

Finally, John blindly picks a chenin blanc and points to it. "We'll try this one."

"Would you like it now, or with your dinner?," Gary inquires.

John indicates that they would like it right away, since Carol still remains undecided about what to order.

In a few minutes, Gary is back with the chosen bottle, two wine glasses, and an ice bucket. After showing the label to John, Gary pulls a wine opener from his pocket, peels off the foil covering the top of the bottle, and turns the corkscrew into the cork. With one hand around the bottle and the other around the corkscrew, he pulls, but nothing moves. He pulls again, but the cork resists. In a last act of desperation, Gary places the bottle between his knees and grabs the corkscrew handle with both hands. He pulls, grunts, and twists, only to deliver half a cork. "Dry cork," he mutters to himself. With perspiration flowing freely, the waiter once again thrusts the screw into the bottle neck. Much to everybody's relief, the cork gives way with a small squeak. As he pours a bit of wine for John to taste, Gary says, "Well, I hope this wine is worth all the trouble it took to open it."

John smiles weakly and nods his approval. After filling the glasses, the waiter places the remainder of the bottle in the ice bucket and asks abruptly, "Now are you ready to order dinner?"

Carol leads off, "Well, I have some questions. I can't decide between the crab legs, the scallops, and the swordfish. Which one do you recommend?"

"They're all good," Gary replies. "It just depends on what you're in the mood for."

Finding no help in this, Carol responds, "I see ... Well, how are the scallops prepared?"

"I don't really know, but I'll check with the cook for you, if you want. I think they have some sort of sauce on them."

"No. That's all right. I'll try the crab legs," Carol decides, sticking with something safe.

John orders his New York strip medium-rare.

Soon after they have finished ordering, Gary brings out the salads with a basket of warm bread.

Long after the salad plates are empty and the bread eaten, Gary delivers their dinners. Carol's plate is piled high with five giant crab legs, with a small dish of melted butter placed in the middle of the plate. The crab straddles a large baked potato. The plate is pleasantly decorated with a fresh fruit garnish. The presentation of John's plate is equally attractive. Quite hungry, Carol and John look at each other with a smile before attacking their meals.

"Can I get you anything else?," Gary asks in a perfunctory manner before rushing off.

"No, thank you," John replies, but Gary is almost out of earshot, anyway.

About half-way into the Pleasants' dinners, Gary glides by and inquires, "How is everything?"

"Just fine, thank you," John and Carol respond in unison. "However," John continues, "we could use another basket of bread, please."

Gary nods and is off once again.

When dinner is over, Gary stops by to pick up the plates. "Can I get you anything else?"

"Not for me," Carol replies.

"I guess that will be all, then," John says, without mentioning the second order of bread that never arrived.

After another wait, Gary returns with the check, which is atop a small black tray. John places enough cash on the tray to cover the total amount plus an obligatory 15-percent tip. The Pleasants depart.

Back in the car on the way home, Carol comments, "I sure enjoyed my meal. Did you?"

"The food was good, wasn't it?," John replies with a vague sense of uneasiness. "But the service was something else again."

"They were a bit slow, weren't they? But they seemed to be working hard," Carol responds. "And whoever decorated that place did a super job, don't you think?"

"Yes, but it just seems they are missing the boat in some way. Something was missing. Something like—well, I felt that we didn't make any difference at all to them. I get enough of indifference at work. It's the 'if you don't like it you can lump it' attitude. Whatever it is, I'm in no hurry to go back there. Let's try that new country French restaurant next time. What do you think?"

"I'm easy," Carol says again.

The Pleasants complete their ride home in silence.

The case of John and Carol Pleasant, although fictitious, illustrates a dining experience that is all too common. You have probably had an experience like this, and some of your customers may also feel they have been treated by your staff with the indifference shown the Pleasants.

The problem at the Run o' the Mill was not its food, its prices, or its decor. These are not big problems at most food-service operations. The weakness at the Run o' the Mill and at many restaurants is the service—the way the customers are treated. As I shall discuss in the next chapter, service is an integral part of the customer's judgment of your restaurant's quality.

Judging a Dining Experience

3

WHAT MAKES a dining experience a high-quality one? How can we evaluate the Pleasants' experience at the Run o' the Mill? How does service fit into a total dining experience? To address these questions, we must first clarify the criteria by which we can judge a dining experience. Four basic factors apply to the customer's judgment of a food-service operation: (1) *product quality*, (2) *price-value*, (3) *surroundings*, and (4) *service*. These four criteria can be used to judge a quick-service operation, a self-service or cafeteria system, or a full-service one (e.g., Run o' the Mill). Before we can adequately evaluate a "total" dining experience, we must look at each one of these areas. None stands by itself, and each affects the others. With this in mind, we'll look at how the food-service industry is doing overall. Then, based on the Pleasants' experience, we'll see how the Run o' the Mill measures up. We will examine the extent to which our operations are providing a quality product, high value, and pleasant surroundings. Finally, we will discuss why service deserves a special place in judging a dining experience.

The Question of Product Quality

As in making any type of purchase, whether in a department store, grocery store, new-car showroom, or a restaurant, consumers look for quality in the products they buy. Obviously, no one intentionally seeks inferior food when dining out. When customers order hot soup, they don't want it tepid. They don't like bugs in their lettuce or bones in their fish. They stay away from sour wine, flat beer, cold eggs, hard biscuits, salty gravy, soggy vegetables, limp bacon, warmed-over hamburgers, stale cake, and yesterday's coffee.

Determining product quality is the first step in evaluating any dining experience. No customer should ever accept or be happy with inferior food or beverages. And, in fact, most consumers generally feel they are getting their money's worth in this area from restaurants. Consumer surveys consistently show that most customers (like the Pleasants) are fairly well satisfied with the quality of food served when they eat out. In the annual *Restaurants & Institutions* nationwide survey, restaurant consumers have consistently ranked quality of food far down the list of common restaurant irritants.[3] A similar study conducted by the National Restaurant Association also showed a positive consumer reaction to restaurant food quality. The study found that food elicits many of the most common *compliments* consumers have about restaurants.[4] Overall, then, the restaurant industry is apparently doing a good job on product quality.

The Run o' the Mill restaurant was no exception. Neither John nor Carol had a complaint about the quality of the food or beverages they purchased there. They enjoyed their wine, Carol was delighted with her crab legs, and John's steak was cooked just as he liked it. In short, the Run o' the Mill passed the test of food quality—as most food-service operations do. But product quality is only the first part of a consumer's evaluation of a restaurant.

The Question of Value

Consideration of product quality must be tempered by a consideration of its price. Consumers want their money's worth from any product they purchase. They try to find the best automobile their budget will permit; they go to markets where they can get the most groceries, nicest produce, and best meat for the lowest price; they shop specials, sales, and holiday promotions. As a group, American consumers are avid bargain hunters looking for that irresistible steal. Whether it comes to clothes, groceries, household goods, furniture,

---

[3]"Tastes of America," *Restaurants & Institutions*, December 1980.

[4]"NRA Studies What Pleases Guests," *Restaurants & Institutions*, November 15, 1979, p. 152.

or eating out, they are always looking for value. They want the highest-quality product for the least amount of money possible.

How is the restaurant industry, as a whole, meeting these needs? Not so well. The *Restaurants & Institutions* survey already mentioned found that a mere seven percent of restaurant consumers perceive eating out as representing a good value. Sixty percent perceive it to be an average value, while approximately one-third rate eating out as a poor value.

These figures aren't as simple as they sound, though. The problem is that the studies do not specify what these judgments of value are based on. They don't tell us what the consumers were comparing restaurants to. They also don't tell us what kind of restaurants these consumers patronize. Are these perceptions related to product value only? Or are the researchers measuring consumer perceptions of environmental value or service value? We don't know.

We do know that it costs more to eat in a restaurant than at home, and this is no surprise. Most consumers aren't cooking for profit at home. Most don't hire cooks or servers to handle their meals, and few shoulder the level of rent most commercial establishments must bear. Of *course* eating in a restaurant costs more than eating at home!

How about convenience? What is the value of convenience to the restaurant consumer? The statistics don't tell us that either. But they do tell us that more consumers are spending a higher proportion of their food dollars away from home every year. In 1984, the typical family spent 26 percent more money on food away from home than in 1980—almost $29.00 per week.[5] Considering the total number of households in the country, this amounts to a hefty $8 billion each month and close to $100 billion each year. There must be some attraction to eating out.

The restaurant industry is one of the few industries today where fair-market economics are alive and well—where consumers "vote with their feet." Competition is keen, and those restaurants failing to offer some sort of perceived value to the consumer just don't stay in business very long.

---

[5]"Tastes of America," *Restaurants & Institutions*, December 1, 1982.

Most restaurants determine prices based on expenses. They tend to operate within the guidelines of 30- to 50-percent cost for an average entree item. This means that for every dollar customers spend in a restaurant, that establishment has already invested 30 to 50 cents in bringing the product to the table. Therefore, customers usually get a lot of product for their money in a restaurant. If they don't, they use the strongest consumer weapon available—their freedom of choice. They will avoid a restaurant that doesn't give them the product value they want.

Value for the Pleasants

The Pleasants probably had a preconceived notion of the value they were looking for. Since they dine out periodically, they were most likely familiar with the going prices for items like those they ordered at the Run o' the Mill. The Pleasants did not complain about the prices at the restaurant.

But the Pleasants wanted more from their evening out than good food at a reasonable price. They went out to relax for a few hours. They needed a comfortable shelter from the demands of everyday living. They wanted an escape and a temporary sanctuary. To determine whether this need was met, we first have to look at the restaurant's physical environment.

The Question of Surroundings

Restaurants generally try to provide a pleasing and comfortable physical environment in which to dine. Although some restaurants spend little on decor, the incredible amount of money being pumped into restaurant construction and remodeling is contributing to an unending array of designs and decors, atmosphere enhancers, lighting techniques, mood creators, color schemes, and environments. It is no accident that the largest single expense in opening a new restaurant is the physical structure.

Each restaurant tries to offer an environment in which customers can enjoy a unique dining experience. They can dine out in simulated south-of-the-border Mexico, turn-of-the-century Canton, "merrie olde" England, or California wine country. If they want a view, they can find it. They can have light and cheery, dark and secluded, funk, eclectic junk, Caribbean soul, country French, live palms, floating gardens, or upper-Manhattan chic. How about mirrors, music, and madness, or a cozy table for two by the fire? Whatever they want, consumers will find it somewhere.

No wonder consumers have few complaints about restaurant environments. Noise, smoke, and unclean surroundings are only occasional irritants.[6] When they do become bothersome, customers certainly do not lack other restaurant choices. On the whole, the industry is meeting the physical-environmental needs of its customers quite well.

Design at the Run o' the Mill

The Pleasants' experience typifies the industry's attention to detail. As they approached the entrance to the Run o' the Mill, John and Carol were impressed by the restaurant's exterior design. Once inside, the Pleasants were equally pleased with the decor. The physical dining environment provided the comfortable haven they were looking for.

But the physical environment of any restaurant supplies only the backdrop for a dining experience. The physical setting can't produce a pleasant meal. A multimillion-dollar investment in a design can set the stage, but it can't supply the acting talent.

The total atmosphere in any restaurant can be generated only through human interaction. Personal, caring service does not grow out of well-watered planters. This type of experience can be produced only by human beings. Design and decor, alone, cannot create a convivial atmosphere. People do that. And when we concern ourselves with the people side of our dining experience, we come face to face with the issue of quality service.

The Question of Service

Now that we have addressed the issues of product quality, value, and surroundings, we can concentrate on the Achilles' heel of the entire food-service industry—service. When customers of restaurants

---

[6]Ibid.

complain, seven out of ten complain about the service. This is a bad batting average indeed.

While we would all agree that service in many operations *is* lousy, the root of the problem often eludes us. We know from the surveys that consumers are complaining about service, but we don't know exactly what that means. The trouble is that we have no firm definition of the word "service," because the term encompasses so many attributes.

When our customers complain about service, they could mean they had to wait an unreasonable length of time for their food and drink. They could mean they were treated rudely or ignored. They could have been rushed, or they could have encountered ignorant or unfriendly servers.

To evaluate service, you must understand what it is. That is the purpose of this book, and the focus of the following chapters.

The Two Sides of Service

Service has two distinct components. Although they are quite different from each other, they strongly affect one another. One side of service is **procedure**. It encompasses the systems and mechanisms for selling and distributing product to customers. It involves communication systems between the dining room and the kitchen. It provides a mechanism by which a customer's product needs and wants can be effectively and efficiently met. This component of service also includes the supervision and monitoring necessary to maintain these systems at top efficiency.

Since the procedural component of service is related to the delivery of product, timing is a major concern. Timing involves both the span of time it takes to get the product to the customer, and the spacing of events—when to take an order, when to follow up on needs, when to provide refills, when to offer additional products, when to clear plates, and when to leave the check. So timing is a vital service skill.

Timing is also one of the restaurant functions over which the server has a great deal of control. As we shall see, proper timing of the various stages of a meal can make the difference between a favorable and an unfavorable dining experience. But so can the other vitally important and often neglected side of service.

The other component of service is what I call **conviviality,** or the service staff's "personality." Whereas the procedural side of service involves the flow of product to the customers, the convivial side of service is interpersonal in nature. Conviviality embodies the attitudes, behavior, and verbal skills that the service person and other dining-room employees display in their interaction with customers. The convivial dimension involves fulfilling customers' psychological needs. It addresses the question of what the customer expects *in addition* to quality food at a reasonable price. It deals with the need to be liked, the need to be respected, the need for social interaction, the need to feel important, the need to be relaxed, comfortable, and pampered, and the need to enjoy the company of other people in a welcoming environment.

From the restaurant's perspective, conviviality is provided when the service crew shows a genuine personal interest in customers. Such interest is displayed when service personnel are friendly, courteous, and enthusiastic, when they show they appreciate their customers' patronage, when they are knowledgeable about the products they are selling, when they use sales techniques tactfully and effectively, and when they strive to meet each customer's unique expectations for quality service. In short, conviviality means that service personnel have people skills.

Service at the Run o' the Mill

The Pleasants wanted a nice, relaxing evening away from the house. For them, dining out was a form of therapy, a way to declare a time-out. Of course they wanted good food and product value, but most important, the Pleasants wanted to have a good time.

Every dining experience begins with reception—with an interaction at the entrance. (Under the worst circumstance, of course, there is *no* reception; the customers wait uneasily for staff attention.) The customer's initial interaction with the receptionist—who represents the entire restaurant—can set the tone for the rest of the dining experience. No start is as effective as a good start. We may not be able to tell what an entire book is like by reading the first few pages but it's a good clue, and the initial greeting at the front door certainly tells us a great deal about the restaurant.

How were the Pleasants greeted? Simply put, they weren't. The hostess, though nicely groomed and efficient, exuded an aura of total indifference. Her attitude bothered John, but Carol, wanting the most for the evening, encouraged him not to let this put a damper on their time together.

In the cocktail lounge, the Pleasants not only had to wait an extended period of time to be served, but when they were finally attended to, the waitress accosted them with tales of woe. Did she express concern for the Pleasants' well-being? Did she extend an attitude of warmth and friendliness? Did she attempt to tune in to their wants and needs? Not a bit. The waitress was concerned about only two things—getting the job done (as she perceived it), and looking after herself. Any concern she may have had for the Pleasants existed only insofar as they fit into her scheme of things.

Like the receptionist, the hostess who seated the Pleasants was indifferent, at best. Her indifference was made clear when she sprinted ahead to the chosen table, leaving John and Carol to find their own way. Her only concern was to seat the Pleasants as quickly as possible.

In the dining room, the Pleasants expected, but failed to receive, timely service. Gary was slow to make his initial appearance. John and Carol waited to receive service for an extended period on more than one occasion (notably between the salad and the entree).

How about conviviality? Did Gary attempt to discern the Pleasants' expectations for the evening or to establish rapport with his customers? Did he project adequate product knowledge and a sense of salesmanship? Did he attempt to make their evening as enjoyable and relaxing as possible? Obviously not. In fact, through his attitude, behavior, and lack of verbal skills, he actually increased the Pleasants' burden, rather than diminishing it. He failed to offer helpful suggestions, he failed to help Carol decide about her order, and when he opened the bottle of wine, he nearly made the Pleasants feel guilty about ordering it. In short, Gary made no attempt to relate to the Pleasants or their needs. He actually provided aggravation when they were seeking relaxation.

The receptionist, cocktail waitress, and waiter were totally system- and self-oriented. They viewed their jobs only from the perspective of following restaurant procedures. In so doing, they completely ignored an essential component of quality service—the relationship to the customer.

These individuals were not malicious incompetents. Most likely they thought they were doing their jobs quite well (and they certainly moved quickly when they moved!). They probably thought they were providing "good service." And why shouldn't they have thought so? They were following the procedures outlined in the restaurant's policy manual. The delays, as I will explain in a moment, were not totally a result of their actions. The receptionist was efficiently keeping the books up to date. The hostesses were seating as many customers as possible. Although overloaded, the waitresses in the cocktail lounge were struggling to carry as many drinks as possible in one trip. The waiter was trying to cover his station in a timely, efficient manner.

But all of these staff members fell short—because no customer, anywhere, should ever be treated with disdain or indifference. Particularly in a restaurant, which is fundamentally a human enterprise, the lack of basic customer relations by any person is intolerable. The service the Pleasants received was abominable. Yet their case hardly represents an isolated incident. The indifferent service the Pleasants had to put up with is alive and well in far too many food-service operations.

A further point: *These food servers were given no reason to change their attitudes or behavior.* After all, they received good tips; John left 15 percent in the dining room and an even greater percentage in the lounge. (Like the Pleasants, most customers also leave full tips regardless of the adequacy of their service.) Furthermore, there was no verbal indication from the customers (certainly not the Pleasants) or the restaurant manager that anyone wanted anything else. So why should the employees behave differently? Why should they be concerned about convivial service?

In the final analysis, the Pleasants actually encouraged the poor quality service they received, because like most customers, the Pleasants left rewards (tips) based on criteria totally unrelated to the quality of service rendered. By leaving a full 15-percent tip for the waitress and waiter, John was unwittingly reinforcing their poor service. But had he left less than a full tip or no tip at all without any explanation, the service personnel would never have known if he was dissatisfied with the service, or whether he just happened to be a "stiff."

The lack of a system for quick, reliable feedback to those who provide customer service perpetuates poor service in restaurants everywhere. As we have seen, other factors contributing to poor service can be found in restaurants themselves. Far too many restaurant operators and managers fail to understand and appreciate the total meaning of quality service (and the consequences of not providing it). Most food-service operators, managers, and employees are trained today in procedural skills, which reflect only a partial perspective on what quality service is all about. Consequently, supervision, feedback, and performance-evaluation systems (when they are used at all) tend to reinforce and maintain levels of service that are less than adequate, as John and Carol found at the Run o' the Mill.

Developing a complete understanding of quality service and its components can help you bring total quality service into your food-service operation. To accomplish this, you need to become familiar with the standards of procedural and convivial service. These standards are explained in the next two chapters.

Service: A Balancing Act of Sorts— The Procedural Side

4

I EXPLAINED in the last chapter that quality service has two components: the procedural side and the "convivial" side. I will discuss the procedural dimension first, and in the next chapter, I will cover conviviality.

You should apply seven criteria in judging the procedural quality of your operation's service: timeliness, accommodation, anticipation, communication, incremental flow, feedback, and organization and supervision. These criteria interact and overlap with one another, of course, but I will discuss each one separately.

The Flow of Service

Service should flow to the customer continuously, steadily, and incrementally. The key to a restaurant's operational efficiency—particularly if it is a busy place—is to maintain an even flow of service. The level of service restaurant customers receive often depends upon the restaurant's ability to establish and maintain a steady flow of service.

Establishing and maintaining an incremental flow of service is more difficult than most of us imagine. Whether it is the taco stand down the street, a giant convention center's food and beverage operation, or a dinnerhouse like the Run o' the Mill, a food-service operation is a complex system made up of numerous subsystems. Each of these parts performs a role vital to the successful operation of the whole system. The Run o' the Mill, for example, relies on the kitchen, the dining room, the front desk, the bar, and the lounge to contribute to the success of the entire restaurant. Each of these parts must work well before the entire system can work well. Moreover, the smooth functioning of each part is dependent on the other's proper operation. The potential for a breakdown in the flow of service is immense. A problem in the kitchen soon affects the dining room and will eventually affect the front desk and the lounge. A breakdown in any one of the system's parts will affect the level of service customers receive.

These parts are in a delicate balance. When this balance is maintained, customers have the best chance of receiving efficient service. When the parts are not in balance—for example, when some are overloaded—the results can be disastrous for the restaurant and for the customers. The Pleasants' experience demonstrates this principle.

The Flow of Service at the Run o' the Mill

The Run o' the Mill's operation was out of balance on the Saturday evening of the Pleasants' visit. Some of the poor service they received can be attributed directly to a breakdown in the flow of service within the restaurant. An hour before Carol and John arrived, the restaurant had been inundated by customers. During just a few minutes, more than 50 guests walked through the front door. The hostess seated all these guests almost immediately. Let's see how all the other parts of the restaurant were affected by this surge in the dining room.

Since all the parties were seated at approximately the same time, and since each party ordered before-dinner cocktails, a mass of drink orders was taken and delivered to the bartender, who was suddenly faced with nearly 50 orders. Setting up all these drinks at once took a great deal of time, especially since the bartender was new on the job. In the meantime, any orders placed after the rush of 50 backed up. Not only did the 50 dining customers wait longer than usual for their cocktails, but the customers who happened to arrive after the rush also had to wait in the lounge for the bartender to catch up.

A similar phenomenon occurred when dinner orders were sent to the kitchen. Since the dinner orders were taken at approximately the same time, the kitchen was besieged with 50 entree orders at once. The cooks uttered a few expletives and got busy, but many customers ended up waiting an extended time for their dinners. In addition, guests who were finally seated in the dining room after the rush was over also experienced an extended wait for dinner.

Since most of the dinners, once delivered, were consumed in approximately the same time, all the orders for dessert or after-dinner drinks were equally delayed. While the parties had finished their meals, their dinner checks were slow in coming back to the table since the cashier was suddenly buried by a stack of tickets to total, by credit-card forms to fill out, and by change to make. Finally, when the first wave of guests departed, they left a flock of tables to clear and set before the hostess could seat other guests who were by now waiting. The cycle was just beginning again when John and Carol walked into the dining room.

This example illustrates how an imbalance in customer traffic can adversely affect the flow of service. Variations of this theme are played out on a daily basis in restaurants everywhere. Furthermore, a sudden rush is only one example of a breakdown in the flow of service. An imbalance in the flow can be generated from any part of the restaurant. Inadequate employee scheduling, equipment malfunction, food or beverage shortages, new, slow, or incompetent workers, and many other unforeseen developments can cause a breakdown in a restaurant's service flow.

With all these sources of potential problems, it can be difficult to establish and maintain a balanced flow of service in a busy restaurant. But without a smooth flow, it is virtually impossible to maintain service quality. The complexity and interdependence of the parts of a restaurant means that an operation can easily "lose its balance" and deliver untimely and inefficient service.

But the balance *can* be controlled. Procedural quality can be maintained if the people who serve customers understand and effectively use the control they have over the flow of service.

Server Control of the Flow

Like most food and beverage servers in full-service restaurants, Gary, the waiter at the Run o' the Mill, has a great deal of control over the timing of certain functions at each table. Because of this, he can direct the incremental flow of service at his own station, and he can influence the balance and flow in other parts of the restaurant as well. Gary can attempt to maintain (or restore) a steady flow of service to each party by coordinating his timing so that the various stages of dinner occur at specific times.

The service cycle at the Run o' the Mill provides at least 13 "contact points" at which Gary can control the timing of his service:

(1) when he makes his initial greeting to newly arrived customers,
(2) when he provides for any before-meal wants such as appetizers or cocktails,
(3) when he takes the dinner order,
(4) when he places the dinner order with the kitchen,
(5) when he delivers the salads,
(6) when he delivers the dinners,
(7) when he checks back with the party to provide any additional service,
(8) when he clears dinner plates,
(9) when he offers desserts or after-dinner drinks,
(10) when he brings desserts or after-dinner drinks,
(11) when he presents the check,
(12) when he picks up the check, and
(13) when he leaves the change or credit-card receipts.

Responsible for five tables, Gary can manipulate the 13 contact points to arrange his service so that each table is at a different stage in the dining process at any given time. It would be disastrous for him, for the kitchen, and for his customers if he attempted to take dinner orders at all five tables at the same time, serve wine at all five tables simultaneously, or serve dinners at the same time, and so on down the list of contact points. If he did try to service all five tables at once, the logjam would create an intolerable imbalance of service to Gary's guests and would also severely affect other parts of the restaurant. But by controlling his timing, Gary can develop a flow of service for his customers that is both timely and efficient.

Timeliness

By planning well ahead and tuning in to customer needs, servers can closely control the timing of the guests' dining experience. They can control when guests eat and drink. They can control when guests leave. They can make the guests' stay last half an hour, one hour, or two hours. They can even influence what the guests eat and how much they spend.

So Gary, or any server, exercises considerable control over customers' dining experience, but the question is how Gary *uses* this control. Does he use it to meet *his* needs (as he did with the Pleasants)? Or does he use this control to provide the timely, smooth service his customers desire? Customers' timing needs vary according to their moods, the circumstances, or the occasion. One party may be in a hurry; another may want a leisurely meal. Gary's job, therefore, is to tune in to these needs and meet them.

Promptness and Other Timing Concerns

One of the direct consequences of a steady incremental flow of service is, of course, timely service. When timeliness is mentioned, usually we think of promptness. Customers rarely have all the time in the world to wait for service. Even if they did, few of them want to wait any longer than necessary. Some of them approach dining from the viewpoint of "get me my food so I can eat and leave." Fast-food restaurants were created to meet many of these quick-dining needs. Promptness is usually a greater concern at lunch than it is at dinner. But extended waits, whenever they occur, are exasperating to most customers.

Promptness is particularly important at the first step of the service cycle—the point of the initial greeting. No customers should be allowed to stand and wait at the front desk without their presence at least being acknowledged. No customers should be required to take their seats in the dining room and be expected to sit there for over a minute without their presence being acknowledged. Even if the receptionist is busy with another guest or in the process of doing something else, and even if the server is busy with other tasks, the fact that customers have arrived needs to be noted and *communicated* to them. A brief "Hello, I'll be with you in a minute," or a friendly nod or smile just to let them know you are aware of them, is essential. Prompt greetings at the front desk, in the lounge, and in the dining room should have top priority among a restaurant's service staff. If not, customers will sit and wait and wonder if anybody knows they're around.

Proper timing has subtle ramifications that go beyond promptness. Timeliness also includes providing service at each stage of the meal when the customers are ready for that service. Gary, for example, has a great deal of latitude and control over the 13 steps of the service cycle at the Run o' the Mill. He must determine the most appropriate time to take customers' orders, bring their salads, clear their plates, and bring the check. Gary's ability to provide timely service depends on his ability to perceive his customers' pacing desires. By failing to pay attention to the pace at which the guests wish to dine, Gary runs the risk of either trying their patience by requiring them to wait longer than they want or, at the other extreme, making them feel rushed and pressured to leave. Whether the guests are eating breakfast, lunch, or dinner, a competent server will note their requirements and provide service accordingly.

Timeliness at the Run o' the Mill

Did the Pleasants receive timely service? After the chilly but prompt greeting at the front desk, John and Carol sat for some time in the lounge without a word from a cocktail waitress. That pattern repeated itself in the dining room. Gary served the salads and bread in a timely way, but the Pleasants had to wait a long time for their entrees. Although the extended wait in the lounge and dining room resulted from a flow imbalance throughout the entire restaurant, effective accommodation, anticipation, and communication by Gary and the cocktail waitress could have immensely compensated for this imbalance. Let's look at these other components of quality service.

Accommodation

While timeliness in pacing requires planning *when* service is rendered, "accommodation" requires planned systems and follow-through on *what* customers will need and want. Accommodation means designing service so that it is flexible and adaptable to widely diverse customer needs. In particular, it means not requiring the customer to adapt to the policies and procedures of the restaurant.

Providing separate checks for large groups is a case in point. Some restaurants refuse to issue separate checks for a single table, regardless of the size of the party. Instead of refusing to meet guests' needs, a restaurant should do anything it is able to do for its guests, even when that is not the easiest procedure.

Other examples of common practices and systems that fail to accommodate guests' needs include these: forbidding substitutions in, additions to, or subtractions from the menu; refusing to make changes or adjustments in orders after they have been placed; requiring customers to make separate payment for different services or products; and routinely refusing legitimate customer requests as being "against policy." Sadly, restaurants that ask their service personnel to respond in unaccommodating ways are reinforcing and perpetuating system- and self-orientation at the expense of responding to customer needs.

Accommodation at the Run o' the Mill

How accommodating was the Run o' the Mill restaurant? Not very. The hostess failed to perceive the Pleasants' need for a place to wait for dinner. It certainly would have been appropriate for her to suggest a place or two where they could wait for their table. However, she was too busy worrying about her own job to worry about their comfort. Once in the lounge, John asked to have the bill for the wine added to his dinner check, a relatively simple procedure. Nevertheless, the cocktail waitress curtly refused. She may have wanted to make sure she received "her share" of the tip for the service she rendered, or perhaps the Run o' the Mill didn't have a system for transferring a ticket from one part of the restaurant to another. Neither of these things should have been John's problem. It is easier for guests to pay for everything at one time, particularly when they are paying by credit card. The waitress should have been willing to handle this request graciously.

Accommodation grows out of an orientation toward customers rather than an orientation toward systems and procedures for their own sake or for the ease of running the restaurant. Accommodation is reflected in the extra willingness to meet the needs of guests in a responsive and flexible manner. Unresponsive and inflexible employees are out of place in the restaurant business (or any service business). When confronted by such employees consumers should do all they can to encourage their departure.

Anticipation

Timely and accommodating service depends on effective *anticipation* by service personnel. Anticipation means that the people who provide service in restaurants are not only one step ahead of customers' needs but also one step ahead of the service flow of the restaurant. If there is a flow imbalance, problems and delays in service can be foreseen and adjustments made. The hostess at the Run o' the Mill should anticipate how many tables will become available and when they will be ready so she can quote accurate waiting times to entering customers. Gary can also anticipate any problems in the flow and adjust his 13 service steps accordingly. Likewise, the cocktail servers can make preparations to adjust the service they provide in response to the flow imbalance. Through astute server anticipation, customers will receive more timely and accommodating service.

Servers can greatly enhance their service quality by perceiving customer needs *in advance*. A highchair and extra napkins already at the table when the family with small children sits down, extra napkins to go with finger food, two forks with a single dessert order, a spoon to replace one dropped by the guest, "doggie bags," matches, the offer of a second cup of coffee—all served without customers having to ask for them—these are examples of anticipation. Servers can go a long way toward improving the service customers receive by tuning in to their needs, not only regarding *when* they will need service, but also concerning *what* they will need.

Anticipation at the Run o' the Mill

As it turned out, John and Carol were victims of inadequate anticipation by the service crew at the Run o' the Mill. The hostess greatly understated the waiting time. She failed to anticipate the delaying effects the earlier rush of customers would have on the dining-room service cycle. The cocktail waitresses misjudged how the imbalance would overflow into the lounge. With some degree of forethought, they could have planned where their presence would be needed most or attempted to find some help from a manager or fellow employee. (Instead, they waited until too late to call for help from the dining room, which was itself overwhelmed.) Gary could have adjusted the timing of service steps with the Pleasants to minimize the glaring gap between the clearing of salad plates and the delivery of their dinners. Furthermore, there was no wine list at the table when John and Carol were seated. This was poor anticipation of customer needs and poor marketing.

Lack of effective anticipation by the service people explains some of the service difficulties at the Run o' the Mill. Proper anticipation would not have made the service flawless, but it would have certainly contributed to a more positive experience for Carol and John.

Communication

Restaurant personnel can have a difficult time anticipating guests' needs unless communication is flowing well within and between the various parts of the restaurant. True communication occurs only when messages are timely (sent and received at the appropriate time), precise, and thorough. Unfortunately, in the realities of the everyday food-service world, achieving this isn't as easy as it sounds.

Breakdowns in communication lead to misunderstanding; misunderstanding leads to mistakes; and mistakes cause inferior customer service. Successful communication, on the other hand, leads to understanding; understanding helps systems and procedures run as they should; and properly functioning systems help contribute to high-quality customer service.

I have a reason for saying that successful communication is difficult to maintain in restaurants. There are four basic points in every communication exchange at which communication can break down. Figure 4-1 illustrates a complete communication exchange, which includes a sender, a message, a receiver, and a feedback loop in which the sender and receiver essentially change roles. Success at each of these four points is crucial to the communication process. If a breakdown should occur at any one of these junctures, misunderstanding will be the likely result. I will briefly explain each one of these factors to show just how easy it is for communication to break down in food-service operations.

Sender breakdown. Communication can break down right at the source—with the sender. Whether the senders are customers, service personnel, or supervisors, the consequence is the same: a garbled message. The sender can cause the following six common communication problems:

Figure 4-1

Communication Loop

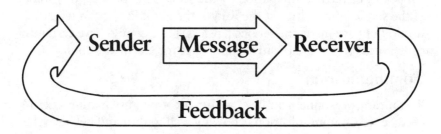

(1) The sender may choose the *wrong time* to communicate (e.g., while the receiver is busy doing something else).
(2) The sender may choose the *wrong method* or communication channel (e.g., spoken instead of written).
(3) The sender may choose the *wrong place* (e.g., the dining-room floor rather than back in the station).
(4) The sender may use a hostile or *negative tone of voice* (alienating receivers).
(5) The sender may use a poor choice of words or the *wrong words*.
(6) The sender's *behavioral signals* may differ from the verbal message.

  Message breakdown. The message itself or the transmission of the message may go afoul. Here are some examples of this problem:

(1) The message may be *too long* to facilitate understanding by the receiver.
(2) The message may be *too short*, leaving out information crucial to the receiver's understanding.
(3) The message may be *too general* or ambiguous.
(4) The message may be communicated *too quickly*, resulting in incomplete reception.

(5) The message may consist of words that carry erroneous or *incorrect information.*

(6) Noise may distort or *block transmission* of a spoken message; piles of papers or clutter may block the transmission of a written message.

Receiver breakdown. The sender may do everything right and the message itself may be fine, but if it is not received, no communication takes place. Here are six common ways messages can break down on the receiving end:

(1) The receiver may be busy, *preoccupied,* or otherwise distracted.

(2) The receiver may *fail to understand* the words in the message.

(3) The receiver may have an *emotional block* toward the sender (e.g., fear, anger, dislike).

(4) The receiver may believe he already knows what the message will be and thus fail to pay *proper attention* to it.

(5) The receiver may be *tired.*

(6) The receiver may be *confused.*

Feedback breakdown. Communication in which messages are sent with no opportunity for the sender to find out whether the message was received (referred to as one-way communication) leads to communication breakdown and misunderstanding. The major culprits perpetuating one-way communication in food-service operations are the following:

(1) Senders merely *assume* their messages have been received as intended.

(2) Senders fail to seek, demand, or otherwise *encourage message feedback.*

(3) Receivers fail to *provide feedback* to the sender, whether it is sought or not.

The potential for communication breakdown exists until senders know that the message was received as intended. Without feedback, the senders never know whether they have communicated or not. This is why communication requires continuous "care and feeding."

Working Toward Successful Communication

Our goal in communication is to make sure the message sent is actually received. But how does this happen? How are the communication skills of good service personnel different from those of mediocre and poor servers? And how do the owners and operators of successful service operations communicate? They employ principles like those outlined below. These guidelines apply to communication exchanges throughout the entire restaurant. They apply equally to interactions between service personnel and customers, among the service personnel themselves, and between owners, operators, and the service staff working for them.

How to Be a Successful Sender

(1) *Make sure your timing is right.* You are wasting your time in trying to communicate if you fail to get the attention of your intended receiver first. The difficulty with timing is that it is relative; the best time to communicate depends on the people and the situation. Asking a fellow employee for a personal favor in the middle of a rush period is a clear example of poor timing. And so is describing dessert selections to customers who are eating their salads. Think about how a server should approach a table in the middle of a heated exchange between the two customers seated there. Proper timing can be difficult, but it is important.

(2) *Keep the message brief.* Sentences and words need to be short and to the point. The goal of successful communication is to express—not impress. So follow the "KISS" method of communicating: "Keep It Short and Simple." For example, how many entree items can the average customer remember if they are recited aloud? Probably three or four, at best. No matter how chic it is to have your food-servers recite the entire menu, anybody who tries to communicate more than three entree items without giving the customer some written assistance is going to experience communication breakdown.

(3) *Keep your messages specific and to the point.* The fast pace of most food-service operations prohibits lengthy dissertations on any single subject. Things need to get done and done quickly, but com-

munication still needs to be effective. So you need to make your message as specific as possible. Ambiguous or general statements can cause confusion and misunderstandings. If a food-server were to announce at a table, "We have a fresh seafood special tonight," what kind of response would she receive? A more specific and useful statement would be: "This evening, we have fresh snapper sautéed in butter for $8.95." It is nice for the waiter to say to the busboy, "You did a good job tonight." But the waiter could communicate with much more effect by saying, "I like the way you took care of the coffees on those five tables tonight without having to be asked." This statement is specific and gets right to the point.

(4) *Use commonly understood words.* We often take for granted words we hear and use each day. But it is easy to forget that others may not be familiar with the same words that we are. New customers, for example, may be unfamiliar with particular menu items. Regional dishes, international cuisines, and wines of the world all have their own technical languages that are not familiar to everyone. Be sensitive to this fact. Look for signs of confusion, bafflement, or bewilderment in customers. They may not know what you are talking about. By the same token, avoid using restaurant jargon too soon with new employees; let a new hire assimilate these everyday terms. Otherwise, you can expect misunderstandings and mistakes to occur.

(5) *Maintain the self-esteem of your receivers.* Messages that attack or threaten a person's self-esteem quickly lead to a communication breakdown, because the receiver's feedback usually involves an ego defense rather than a direct response to the message. Communication is sidetracked thereby, and sometimes permanently stalled. Name calling, putdowns, and other forms of personal attacks will probably elicit a defensive reaction in receivers, who automatically tune the message out and concentrate on protecting themselves. The sommelier who corrects the customer's pronunciation of a French wine can threaten that customer's self-esteem. The manager who personally attacks a food server for forgetting an item at a table during the noon rush is dealing with the situation in a destructive manner. Keep in mind that effective communication is facilitated by nondefensive responses.

(6) *Seek feedback.* As noted earlier, communication takes place only when the sender knows the message was received as intended. Ensuring that this feedback occurs is a joint responsibility of senders and receivers. The feedback must ultimately come from the receiver, of course, but the sender can take the initiative by seeking out feedback; asking for it, demanding it, or refusing to leave without acknowledgement. When receivers realize that senders *desire* feedback, it will occur more regularly. Feedback must be encouraged, reinforced, and attended to, or it will be forgotten.

Feedback need not be lengthy. On the floor, for example, mere eye contact often gives you all the feedback you need. A nod of the head, a lift of the hand, or a quick comment all serve as short-and-sweet forms of feedback—and they work. Of course, more extensive responses are nice if you can get them, but they are not necessary in all situations.

How to Be a Successful Receiver

(1) *Stop talking.* Most of us are poor listeners; most of us probably talk more than we listen. Some people think they can talk and listen at the same time. They are rude, and they are wrong. Receiving spoken messages requires closing the mouth and opening the ears.

(2) *Avoid distractions.* Effective receivers stop what they are doing, when they can, and give senders their undivided attention. If they can't stop what they are doing, they suggest delaying the communication to another time. Drawing, doodling, playing with hand-held objects, looking elsewhere, or just being preoccupied all serve as communication disruptors. So to listen effectively, you should get actual and potential distractions out of the way. Move to a quiet spot where you won't be disturbed. Get out of the kitchen for a minute. Move off the dining-room floor. Get away from the telephone or out of the waitress station. Don't let needless distractions get in the way of effective communication.

(3) *Be an active listener.* Contrary to popular belief, listening is an active process. It requires a great deal of thought and concentration. We fail to listen effectively when we allow ourselves just to receive information. Effective listening—which is done with the whole body—requires mental alertness and an active response. It also requires checking back on the meaning of the communication. Since

what we hear is automatically filtered by our own experiences, emotions, perceptions, mental patterns, and prejudices, we can't just assume we are interpreting messages correctly. We check this by trying to paraphrase the sender's message, or we can ask questions. But whatever we do, if we wish to be effective receivers, we must actively work at getting the meaning intended by senders.

(4) *Listen for feelings as well as meaning.* Many messages are laced with emotional trappings that convey a message very different from the ones contained in the words themselves. Successful receivers remain attuned to these cues and try to bring them out on the surface so the real message can be dealt with.

When a customer snaps at a server, for example, does this mean he is in a hurry, upset about waiting too long, or uptight about something else? An effective server will subtly attempt to find out. When a worker blows up at you for no apparent reason, look for the emotional reasons for the incident. When the food server accuses the owner of caring only about costs and controls, she may really be expressing frustration over an aspect of her job that is not related to money. Look for the underlying meaning in messages. They often have an emotional base.

(5) *Provide feedback to senders.* Let the sender know, in one way or another, that you have received the message and what you understood the message to be. Providing feedback is part and parcel of the active listening process. It may take a variety of forms, from a simple nod of the head to a complete paraphrase of the receiver's interpretation of the original message. One common way of avoiding communication breakdown at a customer's table is to repeat back any order, request, concern, or complaint. This technique provides customers with feedback to the effect that their messages were received as intended, and that some followup action may be forthcoming. If the server's paraphrase is inaccurate, the customer can take the opportunity to send the message again—perhaps with a greater degree of success. Using this technique, you can nip potentially dangerous misunderstandings in the bud, and the customer should receive better service. If more restaurants established a policy of using feedback between service personnel and customers, among the service staff themselves, and between the supervisors and the employees, everybody would benefit.

Good Communication Cues

How do you know if communication is flowing well within your restaurant? Your first cue is the extent to which customers are receiving timely, accommodating, and anticipatory service. As we've seen, this type of service doesn't just happen by itself. An efficient level of procedural service requires effective communication within and between various parts of the restaurant. Here is an example of effective communication: While customers are waiting for their cocktails in the lounge, their table becomes available, and they are seated in the dining room. They are served their drinks at their new table in the dining room without even having to ask. Effective communication between the cocktail waitress and the hostess has made this happen.

Here are a few more examples. When the hostess personally informs customers that their table is ready instead of relying on an overhead paging system, she *knows* that the customers know their table is ready. When customers ask the first person they see to attend to their needs, whether or not the person is their server, and shortly thereafter their server has taken care of their request, communication is working well. When customers are in a rush and tell their server they need a quick meal, and their food seems to pop right out of the kitchen, they have been the beneficiaries of effective communication between the various parts of the restaurant. Moreover, when customers have a complaint or problem at their table, and a manager or supervisor is at the table immediately, communication is flowing well.

The crucial link to quality service is effective communication between customers and the people who serve them. If the message is not received by a server as a customer intended it, or if the message is forgotten altogether, the customer will undoubtedly be disappointed in the level of service. Poor communication occurs any time customers are served an item they didn't order, or any time they order something that never gets to the table. Ineffective communication is also the problem when servers have to ask, "Who ordered what?," when they deliver meals. Any time requests for service are not met to the customer's satisfaction, communication is clogged.

Communication at the Run o' the Mill

Communication breakdown was rampant at the Run o' the Mill, and the result was poor service for the Pleasants. The hostess, who didn't even try to match customers' names with faces, depended solely on the paging system to inform guests that their tables were ready. Not only is this a terribly impersonal way to communicate, but the noise level in many lounges makes reception of "paged" messages difficult, if not impossible. Although the hostess who seated Carol and John knew very well who their waiter would be, she never told Gary that he had new customers. Consequently the Pleasants were left unattended for a long time. Then there was the case of John's missing bread. The refill never made it to the table due to a communication breakdown—namely, Gary didn't remember to tell the kitchen about the order.

The total absence of communication skills at the Run o' the Mill was glaringly evident in the check's silent appearance at the table. The Pleasants did not even hear a simple "thank you." To John and Carol's misfortune, the communication systems at the Run o' the Mill did not encourage timely, accurate, or thorough communication among service personnel or between servers or guests. As a result, the service was inadequate.

Customer Feedback

One important way restaurants can improve service is by actively encouraging communication from customers through a feedback system—in this case, communication not about what the customers want to eat and drink but about their dining experience. A feedback system can inform the restaurant operator about whether customers are satisfied or dissatisfied, whether they want more or want less, or whether they want something entirely different. Feedback allows the restaurant to serve customers better, because the staff hears how it's doing from customers.

Without this feedback, problems or breakdowns may go unnoticed and unresolved. Very often, customer feedback is the first step in uncovering a problem. So whether the shortcoming is slow service, salty soup, an overdone steak, a bad bottle of wine, or a fly in some-one's salad, it is imperative that customers provide feedback.

At the appropriate time in the service cycle, servers should check back and ask customers how their food is, whether they need addi-tional items, and in general whether they are satisfied. (Checking back has the additional advantage of letting customers know that their servers are concerned about their welfare.) Without this feed-back from customers, quality service is nearly impossible.

Servers should realize that many customers are uncomfortable or embarrassed when asked to provide honest criticism. Most people don't like to complain. Why make a fuss about something that's eas-ier to forget, ignore, or not mention? Typically, patrons will complain among themselves, but when the server asks how things are, they say, "Fine!" Others will suffer in silence and never return.

On the other side of the table, restaurant personnel should receive customer feedback in the same spirit in which it is given. Service peo-ple must be receptive to customers' remarks. They should genuinely thank the customers for their feedback. Whether a customer offers positive or negative feedback, the service person should always re-ceive it with sincere interest and gratitude. It is the manager's job to encourage this receptivity for the good of the operation.

Customer Feedback at the Run o' the Mill

Few food-service operations develop built-in systems for obtaining customer feedback. The Run o' the Mill certainly hadn't. No one showed interest in John and Carol's opinions during the entire eve-ning. The Pleasants sat for a considerable period of time in the lounge with empty wine glasses. Nobody came by to see whether they would like a second glass. During their dinner, Gary's question, "How is everything?," asked as he walked by the table, was perfunctory, and not a real attempt to solicit feedback. Moreover, no manager or su-pervisor of any kind came to see how John and Carol were doing.

Both of the Pleasants were pleased with the quality of their meals, but John was disturbed by the attitudes and behavior of the hostesses and the slow service, to say nothing of Gary's approach to opening the wine bottle. But John and Carol had no one to talk to, other than each other—no one with whom to communicate the good as well as the bad. That is one reason that there is little hope of improved service at the Run o' the Mill—at least until the management and employees take an active interest in encouraging customer feedback.

Organization and Supervision

Where was the manager at the Run o' the Mill? Who was supervising the dining room and the lounge? Who was monitoring the flow of service? Who was keeping all the various parts working together? Who was seeking feedback from guests? Who was in charge, anyway? I'm sure customers would say the answers to these questions are "nowhere" and "no one."

Efficient procedural service requires effective supervision. The two work together, hand in hand. None of the criteria for quality procedural service that I have discussed—incremental flow, timeliness, accommodation, anticipation, communication, and customer feedback—will be achieved without sound organization and capable supervision. As we have seen, an efficient restaurant operation requires coordination, cooperation, and integration of all the parts that make up the total system. Restaurants cannot run themselves; all parts of the system require constant monitoring. Employees must be trained and then effectively supervised. When this is done correctly, consumers see the results quite clearly in the quality of the service.

At best, organizing and supervising a restaurant is a difficult job. Since managing a restaurant effectively requires that all the parts be kept in proper balance with each other, we can view the manager's job as akin to that of a juggler. With a great deal of practice, skill, dexterity, knowledge, forethought, and quick thinking, added to some natural ability, the effective restaurant manager keeps all the parts working in harmony with one another.

Supervisor Cues

Here are a few signs of effective restaurant management. First, servers will be relaxed, unhurried, and under control. With clearly established systems and effective training support, the servers' steps will be deliberate, well-planned, and methodical. They will know what they are doing. In addition, they will provide timely, accommodating, and anticipatory service, supported by effective communication and feedback.

In a well-run restaurant, there will also be a manager or supervisor monitoring the floor. Managers must be out "where the action is" to supervise the flow of service effectively. Their job is not just to support the staff, but also to seek and obtain customer feedback. This reflects concern for the customer, and shows an appreciation for the need to gather accurate information so that operational effectiveness can be properly evaluated and monitored.

Quality Service Is Unobtrusive

A well-run restaurant is more pleasant for customers, because they can concentrate on enjoying themselves. Service becomes unobtrusive. It fits so well with what customers want from their dining experience that they are hardly aware of its presence. In the final analysis, efficient procedural service is like an automobile engine. When it's finely tuned and humming along, drivers are rarely conscious of how much work it is doing for them. Only when it begins to cough and sputter or otherwise annoy them are they aware of its bothersome existence.

In this chapter, I have examined the procedural side of customer service. To review, efficient service relies on a steady incremental flow of service, and that flow can easily get out of balance. An imbalance or breakdown in the flow can ripple from one section of the restaurant to another until it affects the whole system—and ruins the service to customers. Nevertheless, skilled servers can exercise a great deal of control over the various steps in the service cycle in an effort to maintain a proper flow of service.

Altogether, there are seven specific characteristics that identify quality procedural service. Each of these service standards provides guidelines we can use to judge the efficiency of the service customers receive. Yet these procedural criteria represent only one side of the service coin. The conviviality of service is just as important as procedure, as we will see in the following chapter.

Service: The Art of Conviviality

5

IF PROCEDURE is one side of the quality-service coin, the flip side is conviviality. Convivial service differs from procedural service in that convivial service is fundamentally human—warm and personal—while procedural service is essentially mechanical. A well-programmed robot could satisfactorily provide efficient procedural service, but convivial service is dependent on human interaction. Procedural service is concerned with the type and timing of service, whereas convivial service is concerned with the *style* of service.

Many of us feel comfortable evaluating the procedural aspects of service, but we are often uncertain how to measure the convivial side of service. Nevertheless, conviviality is a vital component of quality service that deserves our understanding and appreciation. If customers are ever to receive the appropriate level of service in restaurants, we must first understand all the criteria upon which service should be judged. If we don't, our customers will continue to receive the same mediocre or poor service that has become so commonplace.

Conviviality Defined

What lures customers back to certain restaurants and not to others? Why are the Pleasants in no hurry to return to the Run o' the Mill? The answer to both questions lies in the conviviality of the restaurant's atmosphere. Customers will repeatedly patronize restaurants that provide good food, reasonable value, and timely service, of course. But the restaurants that attract the most repeat business are those that give the customer the best treatment.

No one likes being treated rudely, abruptly, or indifferently. Customers want to feel welcome in a restaurant. They want servers to be knowledgeable and helpful. They want servers to tune in to their needs. They want servers to be enthusiastic about what they are doing, and to show that they enjoy serving. They want to see that the server is interested in them. If they have a problem or complaint, they want it handled with respect and courtesy. And when they leave, they want to be glad they came. When customers are treated this way, they enjoy themselves. The conviviality of service is the key to that enjoyment.

Customers are the lifeblood of our food-service operations. That is why it is important to show them how much we appreciate their patronage. The simple truth is that food servers need customers more than customers need food servers. The way our employees behave toward customers tells the customers how much we value their business. This fundamental fact makes convivial service essential.

Convivial Cues

Most customers immediately recognize when they are being treated rudely, abruptly, or with indifference. Oddly enough, though, few people are immediately conscious of being treated warmly. Instead, your customers will gradually realize that your staff is pleasant and people-oriented. Their first clue is usually inside the front door. When customers walk in, they feel the positive energy of a vital restaurant. Employees and guests alike are enjoying themselves. Customers feel friendliness, warmth, and welcome. They are drawn in and made to feel comfortable.

What's contributing to this initial positive reaction? If we were to look closely, we would see that it's not the food and drink alone. It's not the perceived value or the efficiency of service. One's initial positive reaction to the atmosphere in a restaurant is a direct result of how its employees are performing their jobs. Customers, in turn, catch the spirit.

If we were to look even closer, we would see that the restaurant employees are generating this atmosphere by (1) exhibiting convivial attitudes, (2) demonstrating convivial behaviors, and (3) using convivial verbal skills. Attitudes, behaviors, and verbal skills—these are the three key indicators of convivial service. If we are going to understand the full impact of convivial service on customers' dining experiences, we need to take a closer look at each one of these indicators.

Convivial Attitudes

Performing any job involves human relations. Some jobs require more interaction than others, but few jobs depend more on effective human-relations skills than that of a food server. Since the attitudes we exhibit largely determine the degree of success we experience in human relations on the job, the attitudes shown by service personnel toward their customers contribute directly to the quality of service rendered. Employees' attitudes often "shout" so loudly that customers are unable to hear the person's words, particularly in a restaurant. Every move restaurant people make and every word they speak is colored by their attitude toward their job.

Attitudes at the Run o' the Mill

Any restaurant should be more convivial than the Run o' the Mill. If Carol and John were asked, they would probably describe some of the attitudes communicated to them by the restaurant personnel as follows: *The receptionist*—"I don't really care whether you're here or not." *The cocktail waitress*—"I'm tired, and I really don't want to be here. I don't have time to be friendly. What do you expect, miracles?" *The waiter*—"You're not making my job any easier. You can read, can't you?" No wonder John and Carol were nonplussed. Wouldn't you have been?

What a difference it would have made in the Pleasants' experience if the following attitudes had been exhibited: "Welcome!" "I'm glad you're here!" "I want you to enjoy yourself." "I like my job." "This is where I want to be right now." "How can I be of help?" "Can I make any helpful suggestions?" "I appreciate your business." "I want you to come back." "How can we make things better for you?"

The attitudes exhibited by the people who work in restaurants are important indicators of both their convivial skills and the type of service they are rendering. The problem with attitudes, however, is that they are elusive. Attitudes are states of mind, internal feelings, and thoughts that subtly translate themselves into behavior and speech. Attitudes can be known only through their external manifestations—behavior and conversation. Since attitudes are communicated in these ways, a rating of verbal and nonverbal behavior must be part of the evaluation of food service.

Convivial Behavior: Attentiveness

One key to servers' attitudes is the extent of enthusiasm, care, and skill they display in service procedure. The server's care for customers is reflected in the efficiency of service and all its procedural aspects. The more efficiently restaurant procedures are working, the more concern for customer welfare is communicated. When all restaurant employees continually work hard at providing efficient service (and deliver it), they are communicating an interest in the care and well-being of their customers. But this is only the first step toward showing this concern.

Attentiveness is the skill of perceiving what customers need and want. Attentiveness goes beyond timeliness, accommodation, and anticipation in that it requires restaurant people to tune in to customers as human beings. It requires service personnel to "read" the customer and to establish rapport between the customer and themselves. Attentiveness embodies empathy, an understanding of customer feelings and desires. Customers come to a restaurant with varied expectations, wants, and needs. Attentive servers attempt to identify these needs and do their best to meet them.

Reading the customer. Reading customers requires being sensitive to their nonverbal and verbal cues, which customers themselves may not be aware of. Catching these cues helps the service person to be aware of customers' particular needs. This can happen without the customer saying a word. Here are six common nonverbal cues customers might give and examples of how these cues might be interpreted.

Cue #1: **Customer Age**
Small children may need extra napkins, small glasses or extra glasses for sharing drinks, highchairs, crackers or

other items or activities to occupy themselves, and, of course, special menu items.

Teenagers look for inexpensive items, fancy nonalcoholic drinks, and special desserts.

Young adults enjoy specialty items and want to have fun in a casual, informal environment.

Adults over 40 appreciate polite, more traditional approaches to service. It is wise to accord them deference and respect.

Seniors look for smaller portions, less-spicy foods, and economy. They are less tolerant of waiting and, many times, enjoy a friendly conversation.

Cue #2: **Attire**

Customers dressed in *casual attire* are usually out to have a good time and enjoy themselves in a relaxed, informal way.

Business suits can often mean this is a "working" meal, so provide efficient service, but be as unobtrusive as possible.

Formal attire may mean a special celebration that might be enhanced by something the server could suggest (e.g., champagne, a special dessert). Alternatively, such attire may mean the party is on its way to another event and may have time constraints. In either case, check with your customers so that the service you provide will be appropriate to their needs.

Cue #3: **Group Mix**

Groups like special attention. Find out who they are and what type of group they represent. Show that you understand their *group identity*.

A *same-sex group* is usually less inhibited than mixed groups and looks for service that matches its informality.

With *family groups,* defer to the senior member of the family and provide for the needs of any children.

Provide unobtrusive, efficient service to *business-oriented* groups.

Cue #4: **Body Language**

When arms are folded or noses or chins are being stroked, customers are tired of waiting. These are signs of impatience and stress (other signs of *impatience:* customers' looking at watches, looking around, or playing with utensils).

When customers are *looking around,* assume they are looking for you.

Closed menus usually mean customers are ready to order; don't let them wait any longer.

Cue #5: Verbal Abilities

When customers are extremely *fluent communicators,* show deference and respect. If they show exceptional product knowledge, compliment them on their knowledge and choices.

When customers are *less fluent,* or perhaps foreign born, show patience, respect, and understanding. Explain things slowly and carefully.

When customers are *new to* or *unfamiliar with* your restaurant, provide some special help or suggestions. Explain the whys and wherefores. Set them at ease.

Cue #6: Tone of Voice

Customers' *tone of voice* can tell you whether they are relaxed and having a good time, or whether they are uptight, hurried, or annoyed. Listen not only to what they are saying, but how they are saying it. Respond accordingly.

Rapport. Rapport embodies the attitudes, feelings, and relationships that help establish mutual respect between customers and servers. It establishes a friendly relationship. Customers are made to feel comfortable and relaxed. They feel the server genuinely has their interest at heart.

Without rapport, effective communication breaks down, and service quality suffers. A lack of rapport shows in a server who is overly pompous, condescending, antagonistic, or in some way irritating. It also shows when the server fails to take the time to understand customer needs and desires. Regardless of the cause, customers feel alienated from or intimidated by servers who lack rapport. A climate lacking rapport results in the kind of service John and Carol received. Rapport does not necessarily guarantee quality service, but a lack of it most certainly leads to poor service.

Empathy. Empathy is the epitome of understanding other people—putting ourselves in their position, seeing through their eyes, and walking in their shoes. Convivial servers are empathetic. They ask themselves, "If I were this customer, what would I want, and how would I like to be treated?" Increased server empathy leads to greater service conviviality. Servers need not know *all* about customers, of course (that's impossible), but customers want servers to be empathetic to their needs and wants.

Attentiveness at the Run o' the Mill

No one at the Run o' the Mill was attentive. None of the service staff took the time or effort to determine what John and Carol might want from their evening out. No one tried to establish rapport or to view the restaurant through the Pleasants' eyes. John and Carol were treated as objects to be processed—at the servers' convenience. Their human needs—the need to relax, to have a good time, and to be respected and acknowledged as individuals—were ignored, if not out-and-out trampled. It's not surprising that John is in no hurry to return, and that the restaurant left him uneasy. The indifference communicated by the service crew left an indelible negative impression on both John and Carol.

Convivial Behavior: Body Language

Convivial attitudes are also communicated through body language. Communication experts maintain that our body language, which is the silent way our actions and posture show our thoughts, conveys anywhere from 50 to 70 percent of the total message in a typical two-person conversation. Much of the meaning of what we communicate is actually colored by such nonverbal mannerisms as eye movements, hand gestures, and posture. Since body language shows so much of what a person is communicating, we can use our knowledge of it to interpret the messages restaurant personnel are broadcasting to customers.

Facial expressions. The expressions on servers' faces are worth a thousand words. They tell customers whether servers are relaxed and under control or hurried and rushed. Facial expressions are a person's "ambassador" to the world. They silently communicate moods, attitudes, and emotional states. If servers and other restaurant personnel like their jobs, it will show. On the other hand, tense lips, wrinkled foreheads, and icy stares tell customers that things are probably not going well. These negative expressions can eventually tarnish the customers' experience.

Smiles. A smile on the face of a person working in a restaurant is a wonderful thing to see. Usually, however, service personnel get so busy performing the mechanical aspects of their jobs that they forget about the importance of a smile. Smiles tend to get lost in the shuffle of getting things done. Nevertheless, nothing creates rapport like a pleasant, natural, comfortable smile.

Eye contact. Another important body-language cue is whether servers make eye contact when talking with customers. Eye contact by servers reflects sincerity, interest, and trustworthiness. In contrast, lack of eye contact communicates disinterest and insincerity. Nothing is so irritating as having a server approach your table and proceed to look at everything else in the dining room except you. Remember how John felt after his interaction with the Run o' the Mill's hostess. The papers on the top of the front desk were the only thing with which she was making eye contact.

Eye contact is vital in all interactions between customers and servers, but it is particularly important when a problem or complaint arises. The best way for servers and restaurant managers to communicate that they really don't care about a customer's concern is to avoid eye contact. It's a way of ignoring customers, or, at best, keeping them at a safe distance. It's a great defense mechanism, but certainly is a poor way to deal with customer complaints. On the other hand, when servers can look a customer right in the eye, apologize, and promise to make things right, the customer should at least feel better about the situation.

Hands and body. Hands and arm movements are another form of silent communication. When servers cross their arms over their chests, they may be communicating an unwillingness to communicate or a desire to defend themselves in some way. Flailing arms can reflect awkwardness, discomfort, or nervousness. Pointed fingers, jabs, and clenched fists also send negative signals. None of these gestures particularly contribute to the customer's dining pleasure.

Slouched posture or shuffling feet give the impression that servers lack confidence and self-discipline or that they are just plain tired. Confidence and enthusiasm are generated by a deliberate, spirited walk with erect, natural body movements and posture.

Grooming. Another way restaurant personnel show their attitudes of concern for customers is through their grooming. Clean faces, hands, fingernails, and clothes remain the bottom line of acceptable hospitality. Anything less than this is totally unacceptable. More subtle, but equally important, is that servers should avoid placing pencils in their hair or in any way touching their face, nose, or hair. Any behavior of this kind can communicate a noncaring attitude on the part of servers, and a lack of concern by the managers or operators in enforcing basic health and cleanliness standards.

Convivial body language can make the difference between a mundane dining experience and an exceptional one. We need to appreciate and understand what service employees are broadcasting to customers by their nonverbal behavior. When their body language communicates attitudes of welcoming, openness, willingness to listen, and concern for customers' welfare, they are making an effort to provide a convivial dining experience for customers. The clincher comes when convivial forms of silent communication are supported and reinforced by equally convivial verbal communication.

Convivial Verbal Skills

Words may convey 50 percent or less of any given message, but they are still an important factor in service quality. We can interpret verbal skills in two ways: *what* is said and *how* it is said. The what and how of verbal communication reveal a great deal about a person's overall ability as a server, and also about the person's attitude toward customers. Servers' tact in handling a problem, their approach to addressing customer needs and concerns, their use of customers' names, the knowledge they share about the menu, and the help they provide in determining selections all depend in part upon the manner in which sentences are phrased and words used. The ability to say the right thing at the right time in the right way is the essence of excellent verbal communication.

Sometimes the way in which certain words are stressed or spoken takes on more significance and meaning than the words themselves. Attitudes are exhibited through the intonations of the words spoken and the emphasis placed on certain selected words. Identical words can communicate a variety of different meanings depending on vocal intonation. For example, with different intonations, the words "good evening" can reflect any of the following meanings:

I'm really glad to see you.
I recognize you. Glad to see you again.
What are you doing here?
I'm too busy. Don't bother me now.
I'm bored and couldn't care less about you.
Goodbye. Come again.

In addition to tone of voice, an emphasis placed on a particular word within a sentence can alter the entire message communicated in the sentence. For example, the question "May I bring you anything else?" can convey at least four different messages, depending on what word in the question is emphasized.

Emphasis	Meaning Communicated
May *I* bring you anything else?	I want to deliver it myself.
May I bring *you* anything else?	I want to serve you, personally.
May I bring you *anything* else?	I'll bring you whatever you want.
May I bring you anything *else?*	There's really nothing you should need.

Saying the Right Thing

What servers and other restaurant personnel say to customers should be appropriate to the situation. No customer should needlessly be put off by improper grammar or poor use of language. However, appropriateness goes beyond mere grammar. To be appropriate, verbal communication must also be tactful and inoffensive. Moreover, the communication should contribute to customer enjoyment, relaxation, and feelings of hospitality. Customers should never be made to feel uncomfortable or embarrassed by a careless, callous, or otherwise stupid comment from a restaurant employee. Yet sometimes the appropriateness of something said can best be judged by realizing what wasn't said, or what should have been said.

Verbal Skills at the Run o' the Mill

Servers' choices of words make a difference in the level of conviviality. To illustrate this, let's analyze the level of verbal skill used by the hostess, the cocktail waitress, and the waiter at the Run o' the Mill. We will use two criteria to judge the effectiveness of their verbal expression—appropriateness (saying the right thing) and helpfulness (saying a useful thing).

The receptionist didn't necessarily say anything inappropriate. It was what she *failed* to say that made the difference between a warm, convivial greeting and a cold, impersonal one. What she didn't say was "Welcome to the Run o' the Mill." Her job was to make the Pleasants feel welcome. But her poor verbal skills and her lack of eye contact made Carol and John feel as welcome as a pimple on the end of her 18-year-old nose.

Servers should never make complaints or negative comments to customers about their jobs. Sharing gloom and misery is not exactly a server's best method of generating a convivial atmosphere. Most customers have enough worries of their own. Who needs to hear about the problems servers are having doing their jobs? Nevertheless, the cocktail waitress barraged the Pleasants with tales of woe about how hard she was working. Recall her "warm and friendly" greeting: "Boy, this place is a real zoo tonight"? Later, when she delivered the glasses of wine, the waitress complained once again—this time about her sore feet. Carol and John wanted to relax, not to hear about somebody else's feet.

The dining room was no better. Instead of a friendly greeting, Gary started with "Can I get you anything from the bar?" He wasn't willing to spend any time making personal contact with the Pleasants. His only goal was to get an order from them as quickly as possible. Any customer should resent being greeted in a way that is so abrupt and blatantly unfriendly.

Handling Customer Complaints

Another area where restaurant personnel should use appropriate verbal skills is when they are handling a customer's complaint. Any time customers have a problem or a complaint, servers and managers should handle it calmly, smoothly, and tactfully. If the following steps are taken, a complaint can be handled well.

(1) *Paraphrase it.* The employee should repeat the complaint to make sure the message was heard correctly. This effective communication technique tells customers that their message has gotten across. A complaint can't be solved to customers' satisfaction unless the true nature of their concerns are completely understood by the listener.

(2) *Be positive.* All customer complaints should be dealt with in an empathetic manner. Customers should be made to feel that they have the right to complain. The persons handling the complaint should see the problem from the customer's point of view. Then they should tell the customer what positive action they will take to deal with the problem. Customers need to know what's going to be done, and what they should expect to happen.

(3) *Apologize.* The employee should apologize early in the discussion. Nothing is as disconcerting to a customer as having a problem resolved without receiving an apology for the inconvenience experienced. It is also important for the individuals handling the complaint to make sure there aren't any other problems or complaints at the table. Where there's one problem, there are often others. A competent problem-solver will deal with more than one problem at the same time and thereby avoid inconveniencing customers more than once.

(4) *Acknowledge it.* Customers should be thanked for their complaint. Your appreciation for the complaint should be genuine, because the customer has brought to your attention a problem whose solution will allow you to improve your operation even further.

A great deal of verbal skill is required to handle complaints well. But if anybody is well-trained in this area, restaurant employees should be. And restaurant customers should be made to feel that they can speak out any time they receive food or service that is less than satisfactory.

Naming Names

The use of customer names reflects a special caring for customers. It communicates respect for them as individuals. That is why food-service operators need to encourage their staff to use customer names as much as possible. Calling customers by name is a fundamental verbal skill. It is also good hospitality, for it reflects an appreciation for the convivial side of quality service.

Calling customers by name is always appropriate. When servers speak to customers by name, they clearly show they are attempting to relate to them personally and convivially. Servers can learn customers' names from a reservation, from a waiting list (as in John and Carol's case), or from a credit card or check.

No Names at the Run o' the Mill

As is typical of most restaurants, the hostess at the Run o' the Mill did not take advantage of the opportunity to recognize the Pleasants by name when she was seating them; in fact, she again had to ask John and Carol who they were. The hostess could have easily made note of their name and used it in greeting them or in conversation with them. She could easily have passed their name to Gary, and he could have called the Pleasants by name when greeting them at the table, or he could have thanked Carol and John by name when he delivered their dinner check.

Helpful Knowledge

Restaurant employees should provide helpful, knowledgeable assistance when customers need it. When they are purchasing something with which they are not totally familiar, customers seek advice. But customers would refrain from buying a car from a person who couldn't explain the difference between fuel injector and a carburetor. They would probably not purchase insurance from someone who couldn't explain the difference between term and whole-life policies. Consumers want their sales representatives to be knowledgeable about the products they are selling. The same is true of food-service employees.

If service people are going to sell wine, they should know the wine list. If they are expected to sell dinners, they must know what the entrees are, how they are prepared, what they look like, and how they taste. The same principle applies for selling cocktails, desserts, salads, appetizers, and beverages. Product knowledge is a prerequisite to effective service (and selling).

Product Knowledge at the Run o' the Mill

The Pleasants soon found that Gary's product knowledge was nearly nil, and their dining experience was diminished by Gary's inability to help them. He had no information about the wines on the wine list, even though he was supposed to be selling them. When Carol asked about the scallops, Gary didn't have a clue as to how they were prepared. Gary's offer to check with the cook was of no value to Carol. What she needed was an informed person who was totally familiar with all the products available, and one who could describe them in any amount of detail necessary—including how they were prepared.

Product knowledge goes hand-in-hand with the ability to assist a customer in making a decision. Customers often want assistance in making a menu choice, particularly if they are visiting the restaurant for the first time. Customers should consider "Everything is good!" a less-than-adequate comment from a server. Rarely is every selection on a menu absolutely superb. Even if this were the case, the customer isn't helped in making a discriminating choice by such a statement. For this reason, convivial servers will always have a favorite or two to recommend. Whether customers are mulling over wine, cocktails, dinner, or dessert, a little help from servers can go a long way in making sure customers have a positive dining experience.

Making helpful suggestions is part and parcel of convivial service. Restaurant managers and operators usually attempt to encourage suggestive selling by their service personnel. However, most suggestive selling that customers experience is approached with the same lack of delicacy that Gary showed at the Pleasants' table. His selling strategy was to ask, "Can I get you anything else?" As a suggestive sell, this question just doesn't fly. How can customers respond if they don't know what the options are?

Had Gary been a skillful waiter, he could have approached the table after the dinner plates were cleared and said something like, "Are you ready for dessert? We have some wonderful chocolate mousse, or my favorite, deep-fried ice cream." Carol, having a soft spot in her heart for anything chocolate, would have leaped at the chance for mousse. Perhaps she would have split an order with John. With two cups of hot coffee, this bit of indulgence would have been a nice way for the Pleasants to conclude their meal. Gary bungled this opportunity and, in so doing, further diminished his already weak service effort.

Conviviality and Sales

As with any business, a restaurant's success depends on its sales. Without sales, there would be no business. Therefore, it is inappropriate to view service as an end in itself. The function of service is to cultivate, facilitate, and accumulate sales. Service is a means, not an end. If service fails to provide the means to sales, a food-service operation suffers the consequences.

Once we begin to view service as a means of building sales in restaurants, our perspective of service and its evaluation changes greatly. For example, the true function of *servers* can be more accurately stated by referring to them as *sellers*. However, tradition and custom are strong, and the idea that a waiter or waitress's job is primarily to take orders and deliver food remains alive and well throughout the food-service industry today.

Food and beverage servers are the sales representatives for the food-service operations in which they work. Department stores have sales clerks, and insurance companies have sales representatives. Most businesses utilize a sales force of one form or another in order to sell goods and service. The same is true for restaurants.

Effective selling in a restaurant requires human interaction. It also requires that rapport be established between the seller and the customer. It requires a degree of empathy on the part of the seller, so that the seller can understand and meet the customer's needs and wants. This is a basic principle upon which all personal selling is based. In short, restaurant sales require convivial skills on the part of the seller.

Effective selling requires respect, tact, consideration, and caring for the customer. It requires knowledge and assistance on the part of the sales representative. Effective sales requires a convivial approach to service. In fact, the only effective approach to food-service sales is through conviviality.

Restaurant consumers don't want pushy, obnoxious, affrontive individuals serving them. They don't appreciate this kind of selling in other businesses, so why should they tolerate it in a restaurant? They should expect, and receive, tactful, personal, and knowledgeable assistance whenever they make a purchase in a restaurant. When more servers develop a convivial sales perspective toward their job, the level of service will be far superior to that generally found today. Skillful selling and quality service are one and the same.

Any time consumers eat out, they should feel that they have received their money's worth from both products and service. In addition, they should feel like they were treated with respect and courtesy. But rarely do customers experience a truly convivial approach to rendering service. Few servers perceive themselves as sales representatives. Most see themselves as mere order takers.

Food-service consumers expect a level of service that makes them happy. They expect positive attitudes from attentive sellers whose nonverbal behaviors and verbal skills contribute to an overall pleasurable dining experience. The exact method for making this the rule rather than the exception in your operation is the focus of the remaining chapters of this book.

Defining What Quality Service Is for You

6

THE STANDARDS for quality service outlined in the last two chapters provide a general framework for the analysis and evaluation of service in any food-service operation. They can be adapted to a fast-food, coffeeshop, cafeteria, or full-service operation. They work equally well for chain and independent operations, and hotel or free-standing restaurants. Let's review the seven procedural standards and nine convivial standards of quality service.

The Procedural Dimension

You will recall from earlier chapters that procedural service deals with the technical systems involved in getting products and service to customers.

(1) *Incremental Flow of Service.* A proper service flow requires that service occur in regular increments so no one part of the service system (e.g., the bar) is overextended at any one time. This ensures a steady flow of service to the customer.

(2) *Timeliness.* Needless to say, good service involves timing—the time it takes the product or service to get to each customer. Efficient service is speedy. But proper timing has subtle ramifications that go beyond promptness to providing service when customers are ready for it.

(3) *Accommodation.* Service systems and procedures must work for the convenience of the customer. Procedures should be designed around customers' needs for efficient service rather than what's easiest for the operation.

(4) *Anticipation*. Effective anticipation requires that service always be one step ahead of customers' needs. Products and service should be provided before the customer has to ask for them. Timing must be adjusted to embrace what will be happening rather than what has just happened.

(5) *Communication*. Service cannot possibly be of high quality without clear and concise communication between servers and customers, among the service team members, and between the servers and their boss. Messages must be communicated accurately, thoroughly, and in a timely manner.

(6) *Customer Feedback*. Servers must continually find out whether the restaurant's service and products have met the customers' needs and expectations. Feedback helps promote improvement in service procedures by identifying areas of breakdown.

(7) *Supervision*. Smooth-running service systems must be coordinated. They cannot run themselves. The other six procedural components of quality service will not occur without effective supervision and monitoring.

The Convivial Dimension

The convivial dimension of service reflects a server's ability to relate to customers as people.

(1) *Attitude*. One's attitude is automatically communicated to others. When we reflect a positive attitude, other people are attracted to us and enjoy our company. When we show a negative attitude, it alienates other people or can spread, making them feel negative too. Maintaining a positive attitude—which is communicated through behavior and verbal cues—is essential to the provision of quality service.

(2) *Body Language*. Body language can convey up to two-thirds of the message in a typical conversation. Facial expressions, eye contact, and smiles, as well as controlled hand and body movements, communicate much of the service person's attitude toward customers.

(3) *Tone of Voice*. The particular words said to customers are important, but many times the tone of voice communicates more of the "real" message than the actual words themselves. Short, abrupt, hur-

ried, cold, or sarcastic remarks convey negative messages. Quality service requires an open, friendly, and relaxed manner of communication.

(4) *Tact*. Knowing the right thing to say under different circumstances is an important skill for a service person to master. Language that turns customers off must be avoided at all costs. The skilled service person is always tactful and is aware at all times of just what to say or what not to say to promote customer satisfaction.

(5) *Naming Names*. When customers are called by name, they are receiving one of the best signs that the service person is attempting to relate to them personally. Use of customers' names reflects a special caring for customers. It communicates respect for them as individuals.

(6) *Attentiveness*. Attentive service people are tuned in to the human needs of their customers, and treat them as people, not "covers." They know that business thrives on polite, friendly, respectful service. Attentiveness is what personal service is all about.

(7) *Guidance*. Providing helpful suggestions to customers who are indecisive or confused is a way of showing care and concern for them as customers. But before service people can make helpful suggestions, they must have a thorough knowledge of the products and service they are providing.

(8) *Suggestive Selling*. Quality service people see themselves as sales representatives. They understand that business depends on sales and that their job is to sell. They avoid pushing unwanted services and products on customers, but they do attempt to expand customers' awareness of available products and services.

(9) *Problem-Solving*. Customers' problems or complaints should always be handled calmly, smoothly, and tactfully. The message "Thank you for bringing this to my attention" is passed on to the customers in such a way that customers believe their problems, complaints, or concerns are always welcome and will be handled effectively.

Setting Service Standards for Specific Situations

You can use these 16 standards of quality service as a guide to creating a definition of quality service for your operation. This list serves as the basis upon which the service in your operation can be evaluated and eventually improved.

Although the 16 quality-service standards apply to any food-service operation, the emphasis or importance of each individual standard may vary from job to job and from operation to operation. For example, a fast-food operator may rank timeliness and communication as the top two procedural standards and the ability to convey a positive attitude with smiles and a friendly tone of voice as the essence of conviviality for a counter person. In contrast, the most important procedural standard for a hostess at a dinnerhouse might be to set up an incremental flow in seating guests and anticipating service needs in the dining room, while the convivial emphasis might be on making arrivals feel welcome and calling customers by name. A food server's highest service priorities might be communication, establishing an incremental procedural flow, and being an effective, convivial seller.

The standards themselves do not change from operation to operation. All 16 of them always apply. But the weight you place on a specific standard will probably differ from that assigned by other restaurateurs, and it will probably vary from job to job within your establishment.

Setting priorities. Use the work sheet in Figure 6-1 to rank both the procedural and convivial standards for the service positions in your operation. These two ranked lists will be your guide in the next step toward achieving quality service, which is identifying the observable "key indicators" of each one of these standards.

Identifying Your Quality-Service Indicators

After you have developed your ranked list of service standards, you need to identify cues that will tell you whether each of your standards for quality service is being met. Look at each standard on your list and ask the question, "What must happen for me to know this standard is being met?"

Take, for example, the standard of timeliness. Ask yourself, "What are the key indicators of timely service in my operation? How do I know when service is timely or when it is not? What are the specific, observable signs?" To assist you in this important exercise, the 16

Figure 6-1

A Worksheet to Rank Quality-Service Standards

Instructions: Based on the nature of your operation, rank the following standards of quality service in each of the two lists. Put a "1" next to the most important procedural standard, a "2" for the second most important standard, and so on. Repeat the process for the convivial dimension, starting again at "1."

Name of Operation, Job, or Function _____

Procedural Dimension	Convivial Dimension
____ Accommodation	____ Attitude
____ Anticipation	____ Attentiveness
____ Timeliness	____ Tone of Voice
____ Organized Flow	____ Body Language
____ Communication	____ Tact
____ Customer Feedback	____ Naming Names
____ Supervision	____ Guidance
	____ Suggestive Selling
	____ Problem-Solving

standards of quality service are summarized in list form in Figure 6-2, and one or two sample key indicators are listed across from each standard. Although these indicators are provided only as examples and may not be applicable to your operation, they should give you a sense of what constitutes a useful indicator. Remember, indicators must be based on *observable* behavior. They are actions that can be seen and verified by you and by others.

Don't be deceived by the limited number of sample indicators suggested above. You may identify one, three, five, ten or more key indicators for a single service standard. The more indicators your group can come up with, the easier it will be for you and others to ascertain the presence or absence of quality service behavior. Don't expect yourself or any other single individual to generate a complete list of indicators. This task usually requires a group effort.

You may question the necessity of going through the process of identifying key indicators for your standards of quality service. But this is a crucial step in improving service. Specifying the behavior you desire removes your employees' uncertainty regarding your expectations. Telling an employee to provide "timely service" or to exhibit a "positive attitude" is almost useless in the absence of specific standards. You'll be far more likely to improve your service if the desired behavior is clearly spelled out and all parties understand the indicators upon which that behavior is being judged. Instead of merely telling an employee to provide prompt service, for example, you might specify that the employee greet customers within one minute after they sit down and deliver entrees four to five minutes after salad plates have been cleared.

Clear indicators take the guesswork out of what quality service is. Since they represent clear and precise service outcomes, these indicators can be viewed as targets toward which all your service endeavors should aim. When targets are measurable or observable, you will know when you've reached your goal.

The more clearly you can spell out your exact standards, the more effectively you will guide your employees in providing the level of service you desire. To help clarify the difference between a measurable indicator and a vague expectation, the chart in Figure 6-3 (page 88) compares nonmeasurable indicators with observable, measurable ones. The nonmeasurable indicators are of marginal value because they are too general. But when these same ambiguous indicators are rewritten, as shown in the right-hand column, they become a useful guide.

Quantifying some service expectations is difficult, at best. It is helpful to create at least a rough measure of the service indicator in these cases. To assess the intensity of a server's enthusiasm, for example, the manager can establish a rating scale of one to ten (or any other suitable scale).

As an illustration, look at item six in Figure 6-3. The nonmeasurable standard "service personnel exude a high energy level" was converted to a more measurable indicator, a ten-point rating on eagerness and enthusiasm.

Figure 6-2

Sample Indicators of Service Quality

Quality Service Standards	Sample Key Indicators
(1) Service is timely.	—Customers are greeted within one minute of sitting down.* —Food arrives four to five minutes after salad plates are cleared.*
(2) Service occurs in an incremental flow.	—Hostesses alternate sections when seating customers. —Within a section, each table is at a different stage in the total service cycle.
(3) Systems are accommodating to the needs of customers.	—Menu items can be substituted and combined. —Ninety percent of customer requests can be accommodated.*
(4) Customer needs are anticipated.	—Customers do not have to ask for beverage refills. —Customers with small children receive booster chairs or high-chairs without having to ask.
(5) Service personnel communicate effectively.	—Every customer receives exactly the items ordered. —Crew members help each other out when needed.
(6) Customer feedback is sought.	—The server checks back with the party at least once during a meal. —Customer problems and concerns are relayed to managers.

Figure 6-2 (continued)
Sample Indicators of Service Quality

(7) The service is well supervised.	—A supervisor is visible on the floor. —A supervisor makes contact with each table once during a shift.
(8) Service employees exhibit positive attitudes.	—Smiles are visible on employees' faces. —On a ten-point scale, employees receive a score of 10 from their supervisor for being openly friendly to guests.
(9) Servers exhibit positive body language.	—Eye contact is made when talking with customers. —Hands are kept away from faces.
(10) Servers are personally attentive.	—At least ten customers per day speak highly of the service.* —Customers ask for specific servers.
(11) Servers make helpful suggestions to customers.	—Servers communicate complete and accurate product knowledge to every table.
(12) Servers are effective sales representatives.	—One additional item (e.g., dessert, after-dinner drink, appetizer) is sold with each entree ordered.*
(13) Servers communicate in a friendly, personal tone of voice.	—On a ten-point scale, servers receive a score of 10 from their supervisors for friendliness of voice.
(14) Servers use language appropriate to the situation.	—Correct speech is used and slang avoided.
(15) Customers are called by name.	—All guests are called by name at least once during their dining experience.*

(16) Complaints or problems are handled graciously.	—All complaining customers leave happy.

*Standards will vary by operation.

Certainly this form of measurement lacks the precision of time and monetary measures or the specificity of such behaviors as writing correct abbreviations on a dinner ticket or filling a glass of water. Nevertheless, converting nonspecific behaviors to a numerical range is a useful step. Despite its weaknesses, this approach gives you a base for discussion and analysis. Even though your observers may initially disagree over exactly what constitutes a one, a five, or a seven, after they have worked together using your rating scale, their differences in perception should gradually shrink, and they will eventually agree on a uniform approach to measuring service behavior.

When you have completed the worksheets in this chapter, you will have (1) a ranked list of quality-service standards for each service position in your operation, and (2) a list of one or more observable key indicators for each of your standards. Compiling these lists is a large and time-consuming job. But these are crucial steps in achieving quality service; don't cut them short.

Once you have listed your service standards and their corresponding indicators, you are ready to take a closer look at your current operation and to assess which standards are being met and which are being neglected. I will explain how to perform that self-assessment in the next chapter.

Figure 6-3

A Comparison of Nonmeasurable and Measurable Service Indicators

Nonmeasurable Indicators	Observable and Measurable Indicators
(1) Service employees think at least one step ahead.	Customers receive water refills and other items without having to ask.
(2) Service personnel have their sections under control.	Newly arrived customers are greeted within one minute of sitting down and their beverage or food order is taken within five minutes of that time.
(3) Hostesses are friendly to customers.	Hostesses talk to customers while showing them to their seats.
(4) Food servers demonstrate suggestive-selling skills.	At least one additional item is sold at each table.

(5) Cocktail servers are good team players.

The cocktail servers verbally communicate service needs with one another.

(6) Service employees exude a high energy level.

During the shift, service employees consistently approach each table with a ten-point rating on eagerness and enthusiasm.

(7) Service personnel are quick on their feet.

When the food order is ready, it is served at the table within one minute.

(8) Customers are enjoying themselves.

Customers are visibly relaxed and smiling, or at least ten unsolicited positive customer comments are received in one evening.

(9) Service personnel look neat and clean.

Hair is combed; fingernails are clean; uniform is clean and pressed; face is clean and shaved.

(10) Customers are listened to.

The manager personally listens to and responds to every customer complaint.

Assessing Your
Current Situation

NOW THAT you have determined what kind of service you want to provide and how it can be measured, you must assess your current level of service. You need to pinpoint your current service strengths and deficiencies. This analysis should reveal your major service problems, which reflect the difference between the service you want and the service you now have. By the end of this analysis, you will see which specific areas of service require your attention.

If you are the owner or manager of a food-service operation, you probably have some sense of your current service quality, of the weak and strong areas of your service operation. The techniques in this chapter will help you transform this general conception into a list of specific service problems, ranked by how serious they are. The more you can focus on identifying your service problems, the more successful you will be in solving them.

The procedures explained in this chapter will help you conduct your own service-needs assessment. I will explain how you can design and conduct a service audit for your operation and how you can make optimum use of the "Customer-Service Assessment Scale." The audit and assessment scale can help you paint a complete and accurate picture of your service level.

The Service Audit

In their book *In Search of Excellence,* Peters and Waterman write about a management practice found in a number of excellent companies.[7] They tagged it "management by walking around," or MBWA. Peters and Waterman found that excellent companies generally encourage their managers to get out of their offices and communicate informally with subordinates and fellow employees. This activity, the authors found, generates organizational fluidity and allows people within the company to keep in contact with each other. The authors wrote that, in excellent companies, communication networks are vast and informal, promoting a spirit of cooperation rather than one of competition. In such an environment, most managers are visible, accessible, and knowledgeable. These managers are able to stay on top of things far better than managers who remain tied to their desks.

The service audit discussed here is a form of MBWA. The audit encourages food-service managers to get involved in the service part of their enterprise and to get a feel for how the operation is functioning. The service audit, however, goes a step further than MBWA, because it provides a structured format for the walking around. It gives a sense of direction and identifies those areas that require the manager's attention when the manager is out of his or her office.

The first step in conducting your service audit is to construct a service-audit form. Figure 7-1 shows a sample service-audit form for the Run o' the Mill. Notice that this form is simply a series of measurable service-quality indicators. Since key indicators must be specific to a particular operation's needs, service-audit forms will differ from operation to operation. The indicators will also vary among different job functions. But there are two common elements that all service-audit forms should have: (1) a rating scale to record each indicator's frequency of occurrence, and (2) a place to record the frequency of observed behavior.

The audit form for the Run o' the Mill in Figure 7-1 uses a three-point frequency scale, for example. In the small space in front of each indicator listed, the frequency (consistent, inconsistent, nonexistent) is recorded. You could also use a five-point, Likert-type scale (5 al-

(to page 96)

[7]Thomas J. Peters and Robert Waterman, Jr., *In Search of Excellence* (New York: Harper and Row, 1982).

Figure 7-1

Sample Service-Audit Form

Restaurant Name:
Job Function: FOOD SERVER

Scoring: C = consistent
         I = inconsistent
         N = nonexistent

Organized Flow

_____ Each table in a section is in a different stage of the service cycle.

_____ The crew is working at a steady but comfortable pace.

_____ The kitchen and bar are not overextended at any one time.

_____ Customers are not waiting longer than the maximum designated time for service.

Timeliness

_____ Customers are greeted within one minute of sitting down.

_____ Beverages arrive at the table within four minutes after they are ordered.

_____ Entrees arrive within four minutes after salad plates are cleared.

_____ The check arrives within four minutes after the last plate is cleared.

_____ Tables are cleared and reset within two minutes of the customers' leaving.

Anticipation

_____ Customers are asked about refilling cocktails and beverages when glasses are one-quarter full.

_____ An adequate supply of materials and equipment is on hand.

_____ Customers do not have to ask for service of any type (e.g., extra napkins, highchairs for young children).

Communication

_____ Order tickets are filled out neatly, cleanly, and with proper abbreviations.

_____ Servers are clearly understood when they talk.

_____ Servers demonstrate reflective listening skills.

Customer Feedback

_____ Customers are asked how their meals are within two minutes after they have been served.

_____ Feedback is solicited from customers at the end of the meal.

Figure 7-1 (continued)
Sample Service-Audit Form

System Accommodation

_____ Menu items are adjustable to meet customer desires.
_____ Unusual or special customer requests are conveyed to the manager.

Supervision

_____ A manager is visible on the floor of the dining area.
_____ Customer problems and complaints are handled by the manager.
_____ The manager visits each table during the shift.

Positive Attitude

_____ On a ten-point scale, servers rate a 10 on pleasantness and cooperativeness.
_____ On a ten-point scale, servers rate a score of 10 on enthusiasm and high energy.
_____ Members of the service crew visibly enjoy their jobs.
_____ Supportive comments are heard among the crew members.

Attentiveness

_____ Each party is approached according to its needs. This includes:
        _____ Meeting special needs of senior citizens.
        _____ Meeting special needs of the out-of-the-ordinary customer (e.g., disabled and handicapped).
        _____ Recognizing special occasions and celebrations.

Friendly Tone of Voice

Spirit and enthusiasm are maintained in the voices of service personnel:
_____ At the beginning of the shift.
_____ During the shift.
_____ At the end of the shift.

Smiling Body Language

_____ All service personnel meet the operation's grooming standards.
_____ Smiles are visible on the faces of all service personnel.
_____ Body movements are smooth, even, and controlled, yet spirited.
_____ No smoking or gum chewing is exhibited in front of customers.
_____ Eye contact is made with customers.
_____ Hand and arm movements are under control.
_____ Facial expressions are appropriate to the situation.

Use of Customers' Names

_____ Repeat and regular customers are greeted by name.

_____ If a name is recorded on a reservation or waiting list, that name is used to address the party.

_____ When a credit card is used for payment, the person's name is used when the card is returned.

Helpful Suggestions

_____ Servers suggest personal favorites when customers are indecisive.

_____ Servers demonstrate complete product knowledge of the menu (including preparation methods).

_____ Menu suggestions are based on the perceived needs and wants of the party.

Effective Selling Skills

_____ The customers' awareness of items available is expanded by servers' telling about menu items.

_____ When suggesting a particular item, the server tells the features and the benefits of that item.

_____ A customer's price range is recognized and respected.

Tactful Words

_____ Proper etiquette is exhibited by all service personnel.

_____ Correct language and grammar are heard in the dining room.

_____ Slang is avoided among the service crew.

_____ Restaurant jargon is avoided in front of customers.

_____ Friction is avoided among fellow employees.

Gracious Problem-Solving

_____ Complaining customers leave happy.

_____ Managers make contact with all complaining customers.

_____ Solutions to problems are appropriate to the problem, as indicated by each customer's appreciation of the solution.

ways, 4 usually, 3 sometimes, 2 rarely, 1 never—this works equally well with a seven-point scale or a ten-point scale). To use the service-audit form effectively,however, you *must* record some sort of frequency measure.

As you can see, conducting the service audit requires MBWA. Auditing service requires careful scrutiny of each service step and function. Performing a service audit helps food-service managers look at the right things and talk about the right things, as well as reinforcing and rewarding the behavior that generates quality service.

The service audit can be used for observing an entire service operation, specific work group (e.g., lunch food servers), or a single individual. Regardless of the group or number of people you are observing, the audit form should be used as a basis for discussion and analysis. Throughout the audit, observers should maintain an analytical frame of reference, rather than one of blame. To limit emotional reactions, several managers could fill out the audit form and compare their results. The management team's results can be tallied and a list of major strengths and weaknesses developed. Credit, recognition, and reward should be given for appropriate service behavior, for when it comes to improving behavior in service personnel, a "pat on the back" is far more effective than a "kick in the butt."

A dangerous misuse of the service audit is to go out on the floor merely to criticize. This approach to the service audit will soon turn any effort to improve service into a disaster. It is far more effective to catch service employees doing something right than to harp on what they are doing wrong. The service audit is designed to help managers become more aware of strong service areas, as well as weak ones. Use the service audit to reinforce the behavior you want. Be positive and encouraging. This is the spirit of MBWA.

If you do use the service audit as a means of finding fault and casting blame, you will establish a climate of distrust and cut off communication. Without a trusting and supportive climate, your efforts to change your service staff's behavior will probably fail.

When you notice that some indicators occur only infrequently, flag them for now, but act only after strategies for improvement have been formulated. (In chapters 8 and 9, I will explain exactly how you can do this.)

The Customer-Service Assessment Scale

The Customer-Service Assessment Scale (CSAS) is another useful tool for assessing the adequacy of current customer service. The complete scale is found at the end of this chapter. The CSAS is a needs-analysis and problem-identification instrument that consists of 40 items describing certain characteristics of customer-service operations. Half of the items are procedural, and the other half relate to service's convivial dimension. Using a six-point rating scale, you measure how frequently your employees (or other target group or individual) exhibit each desirable service behavior.

After the CSAS is completed for the group or individual, responses are tallied and recorded on a matrix. This graph is the service configuration for the group or individual under consideration (examples are shown in Figures 7-2 through 7-5). This matrix's configuration is referred to as the arena of service quality. The arena's shape gives a general interpretation of the level of service provided by the group or individual. Furthermore, specific analysis of the responses to each item on the CSAS can reveal your service strengths and weaknesses in a detailed fashion.

Four Basic Service Arenas

Four basic patterns emerge from plotting the CSAS responses on a graph. The patterns of these four arenas of service quality are: (1) the "freezer," (2) the "factory," (3) the "friendly zoo," and (4) the "full balance."

The **freezer** is a limited service arena of *poor procedure* and *meager conviviality*. As shown in Figure 7-2, the small size of this service arena leaves a great deal of room for improvement. These operations (like the Run o' the Mill) provide inadequate procedural service that is hardly convivial. Because the service is slow, inconsistent, and disorganized, the customers at these restaurants experience a great deal of inconvenience and frustration. Worse, the service staff is generally insensitive to the customers' frustrations, conveying an attitude that is impersonal and aloof. Servers communicate no sense of interest to the customer and broadcast this silent message: "We don't really care about you."

Figure 7-2

The Freezer—A Limited Arena

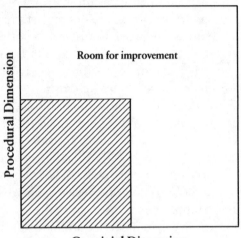

Service Characteristics:	Procedural	Convivial
	slow	insensitive
	inconsistent	cold or impersonal
	disorganized	apathetic
	chaotic	aloof
	inconvenient	uninterested

Message to customers: "We don't care."

The service at **factory operations** is skewed strongly toward *procedural efficiency* (Figure 7-3). These restaurants are doing at least some things right. I say they are procedurally skewed because their service is timely and efficient, but their employees are cold. This configuration leaves a great deal of room for improvement in the convivial dimension. Service may be fast and efficient, but it's also unfriendly and insensitive to customers' personal needs. This type of service conveys this message to the customer: "You are a number. We are here to process you as efficiently as we can."

Figure 7-3

The Factory— Skewed Toward Procedure

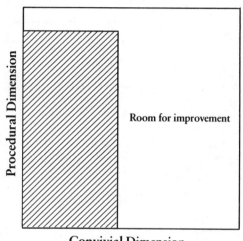

Service Characteristics:

	Procedural	Convivial
	timely	insensitive
	efficient	apathetic
	uniform	aloof
		uninterested

Message to customers: "You are a number. We are here to process you."

The **friendly zoo** (Figure 7-4) is skewed toward *convivial warmth*, the other extreme. While service is friendly, personal, and warm, it is also slow, inconsistent, and disorganized. Service people may show a great deal of interest in their customers and be tactful and polite, but the inconvenience of procedural problems often overshadows all the "warm fuzzies" the staff provides. (We frequently see this kind of service in newly opened restaurants run by inexperienced operators.) The message to the customer from this kind of service is, "We are trying hard, but we don't really know what we are doing."

Figure 7-4

The Friendly Zoo—
Skewed Toward Conviviality

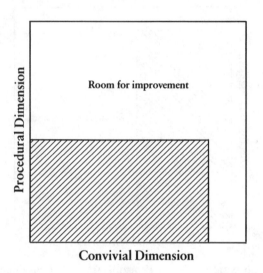

Service Characteristics:	Procedural	Convivial
	slow	friendly
	inconsistent	personable
	disorganized	interested
	chaotic	tactful
	inconvenient	

Message to customers: "We are trying hard, but we don't really know what we're doing."

Of course, what we should be striving for in our food-service operations is a service configuration as close as possible to the **full balance,** in which *both dimensions are well-matched,* an arena shown in Figure 7-5. Even though I call this a full arena, the graph still reflects some possibility for improvement, since perfection is rare. On

Figure 7-5

The Full Balance—
Approaching Perfection

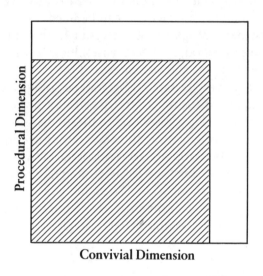

Convivial Dimension

Service Characteristics:	Procedural	Convivial
	timely	friendly
	efficient	personable
	uniform	interested
		tactful

Message to customers: "We care, and we deliver!"

the whole, however, the procedural and convivial dimensions are well-handled in this operation. With regard to procedure, service is timely, efficient, and uniform—consistently good. The service is also convivial; the service personnel have a friendly, personal approach. They also show a real interest in customers as individuals. To the customer, the message is, "We care about you, and we deliver."

Using the Customer Service Assessment Scale

The application of the CSAS is very flexible. It can be used to rate an individual or a group. It can be used for self-evaluation or for rating others. It can be used by an individual to obtain input from others regarding his or her individual service abilities. It can be used by managers to receive feedback about themselves or to give feedback to their service personnel. Likewise, it can be filled out by service personnel to provide feedback to themselves or to their managers. Regardless of its application, the CSAS's usefulness lies in the ability to expose service strengths and weaknesses.

Self-assessment. Service supervisors and personnel alike can gain insight into their own customer-service behavior by completing the CSAS for themselves. Their responses to the 40 items will generate a personal service configuration and show areas needing improvement. In addition, their responses on each of the individual items will help pinpoint their personal service assets and liabilities. Individual items receiving a low rating (0 or 1) should be given attention. The employee can list these problem areas in order of importance so that the individual can focus on improving the highest priority problems first.

Assessment by others. Self-evaluation serves as a useful tool for an individual's own professional development, but it is often biased by the difficulties of self-perception. Our self-perception is usually filtered by our experiences and ego. That is why our self-evaluation is usually different from someone else's evaluation of us. Asking others to rate us on the CSAS provides valuable information, because it tells us how we are coming across to others. This helps us see ourselves as others see us. All in all, this process provides worthwhile insight into our service skills.

Managers' assessment. Restaurant managers can ask their service employees to complete a CSAS self-evaluation, while the manager fills out one for each employee. Then the manager can compare responses with each employee. This process works best in an atmosphere of openness, trust, and respect. Similarities and differences in responses can be discussed. From this session, the boss and employee can develop a third scale that represents a mutual agreement regarding the employee's service behavior.

Supervisors' self-assessment. Supervisors can also evaluate their own service strengths and weaknesses by using the CSAS. After they do that, they should ask their employees to rate them on the same scale. To ensure objective responses, employee assessments should be kept anonymous. A supervisor will get more honest responses from employees when they don't have to worry about recriminations over their feedback to the boss.

After receiving the responses from the service crew, managers can tally the results to create a "composite service configuration." They can then compare this configuration with one based on their own evaluations. This comparison will provide valuable feedback to the managers on how they are being perceived by their service personnel. Using these data, managers can make a list of their major service problems—the areas that consistently received low scores on the CSAS. Problem areas should be listed in order of priority and solved one at a time.

Group analysis. When using the CSAS for group analysis and problem-solving, respondents should be asked to rate the group as a whole. Individual respondents may be indirectly rating themselves as a member of the group in question, but it is the entire group, not the individual, that must be considered. This means that the respondents should "average" the sum of individual service behavior within the group or imagine a "total group" service rating for each of the 40 items on the scale.

Group analysis for managers. The supervisory group can apply this technique to themselves, responding to the scale for themselves *as a group*. Their ratings of the group can then be tallied and compared with one another. Again, a complete configuration can be drawn for these combined responses, providing another perspective of the group's service strengths and weaknesses. Individual items can be analyzed to determine the reasons for different perceptions and responses. When this process is combined with friendly discussion and analysis, it can serve as a useful tool for exposing service-skill deficiencies among the management team members. And when this rating is compared to the service employees' ratings of the management team, a relatively complete view can be constructed of the management team's service-skill assets and liabilities. This is a crucial step in the process of improving customer service.

Group analysis for servers. When analyzing the behavior of various service groups (e.g., food servers, cocktail servers, buspersons, bartenders), everyone in the group should be asked to fill out the CSAS for his or her particular group. Buspersons respond for buspersons, food servers for food servers, and so on. Furthermore, responding employees must be asked to rate only the group working their shift. The lunch crew and the dinner crew, for example, will need separate analytical sessions if the individual members of these groups don't work with each other. Furthermore, respondents must be familiar with the group members to respond appropriately, so the group members should have worked together for some time.

One of the most constructive ways to analyze the group's results is for the group members themselves to discuss their individual responses and generate a list of what they consider to be their top five or six major service deficiencies.

This procedure works best in groups of five to seven persons. When groups are larger than this, divide them into subgroups. Smaller groups facilitate discussion and give all group members a chance to make suggestions and give their point of view. Once the specific groups are defined, the name or description of each group should appear on the top of each completed scale coming from that group. The names of individual group members are usually not necessary. In fact, responses will be more candid when individual names are left off the form.

The result should be a definitive list of service deficiencies for a given service group, generated by the group itself. This process usually works well, because the people actually performing the service are provided an opportunity to analyze their own service behavior. They become active participants in their own professional improvement. They have the chance to take an objective view of the service they are providing and to discover how the others in their group see things. Participants are usually less defensive and resistant to subsequent changes in service behavior as a result of participating in the CSAS process. In fact, the group's commitment to improving the operation's customer service should be enhanced.

Use of the CSAS provides an opportunity for crew members to see what they are doing right and to see where their strengths lie. As a result, their confidence should increase, and they should be more aware of the behavior that translates directly into quality service.

After Assessment, What?

In this chapter, I have suggested two major ways to obtain an objective assessment of your operation's current service standards. The service audit is tailor-made to encourage managers to observe the service area and watch for key indicators of quality service. It encourages MBWA and strengthens the communication process between you and your service personnel. The CSAS facilitates self-awareness of individual service behavior and also serves as a valuable tool for group analysis and problem-solving. It provides an opportunity for service groups to map out their own route to improving customer-service skills, and it encourages the active participation of managers and service personnel alike.

The product of these assessment steps will be a list of service deficiencies that demand the attention of you and your staff. These problem areas should be listed in order of priority so that your major problems can be dealt with first. Once these top problems are identified, your next step is to generate possible solution strategies to deal with them. That is the topic of the next chapter.

Customer-Service Assessment Scale (CSAS)

Name of Individual or Group _____

With this individual in mind, answer the following questions according to how often the behavior *actually* occurs.	Always	Usually	Fairly often	Occa-sionally	Rarely	Never
Does this person or group:						
(1) Provide service in a timely manner consistent with customer needs?	5	4	3	2	1	0
(2) Display bad moods on the job?	0	1	2	3	4	5
(3) Make service as convenient as possible for customers?	5	4	3	2	1	0
(4) Approach customers in a pleasant way even if they are not easy to deal with?	5	4	3	2	1	0
(5) Anticipate service needs before the customer has to ask for service?	5	4	3	2	1	0
(6) Keep hands, face, body, and clothing clean and tidy?	5	4	3	2	1	0
(7) Convey attitudes of warmth and friendliness to customers?	5	4	3	2	1	0
(8) Communicate with customers in a timely, accurate, and thorough manner?	5	4	3	2	1	0
(9) Communicate with other crew members in a timely, accurate, and thorough manner?	5	4	3	2	1	0

	Always	Usually	Fairly often	Occa-sionally	Rarely	Never
(10) Display enthusiasm toward the job?	5	4	3	2	1	0
(11) Seek feedback from customers?	5	4	3	2	1	0
(12) Allow customers to feel neglected in the rush of other activities?	0	1	2	3	4	5
(13) Operate effectively without a great deal of supervision?	5	4	3	2	1	0
(14) Make eye contact with customers when talking with them?	5	4	3	2	1	0
(15) Greet customers immediately when they approach the service area, regardless of the volume of business?	5	4	3	2	1	0
(16) Deal with customers in an aloof or condescending way?	0	1	2	3	4	5
(17) Follow procedures that encourage an even flow of service to customers?	5	4	3	2	1	0
(18) Tailor service to the specific needs of customers?	5	4	3	2	1	0
(19) Know and deal with service needs in order of priority?	5	4	3	2	1	0
(20) Allow a smile to get lost in the shuffle of getting things done?	0	1	2	3	4	5
(21) Make sure there are enough supplies and equipment available to support customer service?	5	4	3	2	1	0

Customer Service Assessment Scale
(continued)

		Always	Usually	Fairly often	Occa-sionally	Rarely	Never
(22)	Chew gum or use tobacco within sight of customers?	0	1	2	3	4	5
(23)	Participate in the evaluation of individual or group customer-service skills?	5	4	3	2	1	0
(24)	Provide that "extra touch" when serving customers?	5	4	3	2	1	0
(25)	Participate in service-skill training?	5	4	3	2	1	0
(26)	Use voice intonations that are warm and welcoming with customers?	5	4	3	2	1	0
(27)	Attend meetings to upgrade service skills?	5	4	3	2	1	0
(28)	Communicate personal or job-related problems to customers?	0	1	2	3	4	5
(29)	Use feedback from customers to improve quality of service?	5	4	3	2	1	0
(30)	Handle complaints graciously and to the customer's satisfaction?	5	4	3	2	1	0
(31)	Take actions to correct problems that consistently cause customer complaints?	5	4	3	2	1	0
(32)	Provide helpful suggestions to customers?	5	4	3	2	1	0
(33)	Deal personally with customer-related problems?	5	4	3	2	1	0

	Always	Usually	Fairly often	Occasionally	Rarely	Never
(34) Exhibit a thorough knowledge of all available products and services?	5	4	3	2	1	0
(35) Participate in the customer-service training of new crew members?	5	4	3	2	1	0
(36) Call customers by name?	5	4	3	2	1	0
(37) Participate in the customer-service training of supervisors?	5	4	3	2	1	0
(38) Use offensive or sarcastic language when dealing with customers?	0	1	2	3	4	5
(39) Participate in efforts to improve selling skills?	5	4	3	2	1	0
(40) Use effective selling skills?	5	4	3	2	1	0

CSAS Scoring, next page. ☛

CSAS Scoring

Scoring Instructions: Record your response for each item in the designated space below. Odd-numbered items reflect your responses on the procedural dimension and even-numbered items reflect your responses on the convivial dimension.

Procedural dimension		Convivial dimension	
1 _____	21 _____	2 _____	22 _____
3 _____	23 _____	4 _____	24 _____
5 _____	25 _____	6 _____	26 _____
7 _____	27 _____	8 _____	28 _____
9 _____	29 _____	10 _____	30 _____
11 _____	31 _____	12 _____	32 _____
13 _____	33 _____	14 _____	34 _____
15 _____	35 _____	16 _____	36 _____
17 _____	37 _____	18 _____	38 _____
19 _____	39 _____	20 _____	40 _____
Procedural total _____		**Convivial total** _____	

Plot total score on the graph below. Extend the *procedural* score point **across** the grid and *convivial* score point **up** until both lines cross. The area inside these two lines represents the "arena" of service quality for the group or individual being scored (see p. 97).

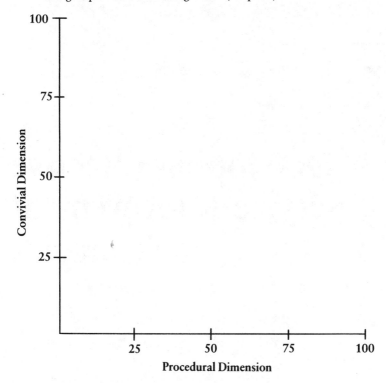

Developing Effective Service-Improvement Strategies

8

NOW THAT you have identified your customer-service problems and have placed them in order of priority, you should turn to developing the most effective strategy or set of strategies to solve the problems. Your first step is to analyze each problem area carefully. You must look at the forces that are working in your favor, as well as those forces that oppose you. Once you have uncovered these vital factors, you can generate a list of strategies to counteract the negative factors and to reinforce the positive. Examine as many alternative solution strategies as possible. By doing so, you increase your chances of choosing the best possible solutions for your service problems.

In this chapter, I will discuss a method of developing solutions to your service deficiencies that should work well for you. This method has three steps: (1) analyzing each problem area using the "force-field analysis" technique, (2) generating a variety of possible solution alternatives, and (3) choosing the "best" solution strategies for your situation. Since many of your solution strategies will undoubtedly require an improvement in your service training, I will outline a number of innovative training alternatives for both personnel and managers.

Force-Field Analysis

Force-field analysis is a way of examining forces working for you and against you in the accomplishment of a given goal. (Figure 8-1 shows a diagram of the force-field concept.) The technique is based on a model that explains a given state of affairs in an organization as a

Figure 8-1

Generic Diagram of Force-Field Analysis

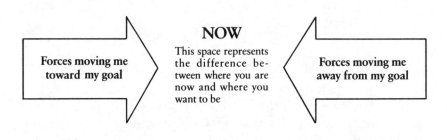

balancing of opposing forces—those pushing toward goal achievement and those pushing away from that goal. In your operation some forces are moving you closer to what you want to accomplish, and some are pushing you farther away. At any given time, these positive and negative forces establish a sort of equilibrium, but this balance may not be at the point where you want to be.

The opposing forces are constantly at play. The greater the negative forces, the wider the disparity between your goal and your current situation. The greater the positive forces, the closer you move toward your goal. But if the negative forces are particularly strong, you can exert a great deal of energy without moving much closer to your goal. That is why effective solution strategies must *eliminate or reduce* negative forces. Merely reinforcing or building up positive forces in an attempt to "overpower" the negative forces rarely generates significant progress toward goal achievement, and this activity can create a great deal of organizational turmoil and conflict. Therefore, the object of a strategy for change should be one of reducing the resisting forces or converting them to positive forces. By reducing or converting negative forces, you will certainly move closer to reaching your desired goal.

Forces at the Run o' the Mill

A sample force-field analysis for the Run o' the Mill restaurant is shown in Fig. 8-2. As we have seen, its service employees lack the product knowledge and training that would make them effective sales representatives. As a result, both service and sales are suffering. A goal for the Run o' the Mill, therefore, is to increase sales and improve service by expanding the service crew's product knowledge and suggestive-selling skills. We already know what kind of experience John and Carol Pleasant had at the Run o' the Mill, but the force-field analysis provides added insight into why the problems occurred in the first place. The force-field analysis graphically shows that the restaurant is a long way from its desired goal. The negative forces are overpowering, and the positive factors are minimal. Furthermore, things are not going to get any better at the Run o' the Mill until the management staff systematically reduces or eliminates the negative forces. The first step in doing that is to generate as many solution ideas as possible.

Generating Solution Alternatives

Solution strategies at the Run o' the Mill—and in your operation— should be chosen with care. The first idea that comes to mind for solving a particular problem is not always the best one. But when an array of solution alternatives is available, the chances of finding a strategy that will succeed are increased. Comparing and contrasting alternatives helps uncover the solution that best fits an individual operation.

Better solutions grow out of an investigation of the options available. There are two essential ways to bring your options to light. One is brainstorming, and the other is keeping abreast of what's going on within the food-service industry.

Brainstorming. The brainstorming process is a group activity based on the adage "two heads are better than one." Ideas from one group member stimulate ideas in another. To start, assign one person the job of recording all ideas generated, and then ask the group to suggest ideas for possible solutions. The goal is to come up with as many ideas as possible, so participants' imaginations should be given free rein. In brainstorming, any idea is acceptable. Don't stop to an-

Figure 8-2

Force-Field Analysis

Situation: The Run o' the Mill restaurant wants to begin a program that will help improve sales and customer service at the same time. Management has discovered that one of the weakest service areas among the crew is product knowledge and selling skills. The manager's analysis might look as follows.

Forces moving me toward my goal

1. The crew, on the whole, is competent and knows how to do its job as currently defined.
2. The crew is experienced. Average length of service is one year.
3. There is a desire among the service crew to increase tips.
4. The managers are committed to working with servers on their selling skills and product knowledge.
5. The service crew holds regular biweekly meetings to discuss problems and scheduling.
6. There are several "natural" salespersons among the crew.
7. The crew has shown the ability to sell during a two-week wine-selling contest.

Forces moving me away from my goal

1. There are no programs or materials for upgrading the skills of experienced employees.
2. There is a lack of written information about our menu items and wines.
3. There is no testing program to assess the crew's product knowledge.
4. Several crew members have a "know-it-all" attitude.
5. There has been no previous long-term managerial push to improve selling effectiveness among the crew.
6. No service-evaluation and feedback system exists.
7. We have a new wine list, and most of the crew is unfamiliar with it.
8. There is currently poor communication between the kitchen and the service crew about the daily specials.
9. There has been no previous training in suggestive selling skills.

alyze or criticize a particular suggestion during the session, or you may shut off creativity and discourage innovative suggestions.

The time to begin analyzing the ideas is *after* the group can come up with no additional ideas and suggestions. The ideas with the greatest promise can then be discussed further. Ultimately, one or more of those suggestions will probably be chosen to solve your particular service problems.

Industry trends. Next to group brainstorming, the best way to gain exposure to a wide variety of alternatives for improving your customer service is to find out what others are doing. Acquaint yourself with periodicals, articles, and books on the subject of service, and be active in your state association and the National Restaurant Association. You can also attend conferences and workshops. Discover what the competition is doing. Know your options. Remember, the objective at this stage is not necessarily to make a decision, but to accumulate a wealth of alternative strategy solutions. Once you are satisfied that you have identified all your alternatives, you can begin the process of choosing your solutions.

Making the Choice

The choice of an appropriate solution strategy is yours, but choose carefully. Pick a solution that fits you, your operation, and your people. Choose a strategy that you can afford and that you can "try on for size" before committing yourself completely. You may be helped by considering the following solution criteria before making your final decision.

• Your solution strategy should be *sound* in principle. You should attempt to solve your service difficulties with strategies that are based on sound principles of management and organizational behavior. Look for solutions that have been used successfully elsewhere. Get accurate reports from those who have applied the strategy regarding its strong and weak points. Above all, avoid fads and fly-by-night remedies that fail to reflect solid research and practical applications.

• Your solution strategy should have a *positive effect* on performance and productivity. Your solution should increase the performance of your service personnel, rather than inhibiting or otherwise adversely affecting their performance. Will productivity be enhanced or reduced? What are the short-term as well as long-term effects? Avoid making the mistake of gaining a few short-term successes that lead to long-term losses.

• Your solution strategy should be *cost-effective*. Are you getting the most for your money? Can you figure a reasonable return on the investment required for your strategy? Is this the best alternative for you at this time? If you are not going to get your money's worth, discard the idea.

• Your solution strategy should be *compatible* with your existing systems and ways of doing business. Shy away from solutions that require major operational changes in favor of those that fit in well with existing policies and procedures. Is the contemplated change consistent with your operation's culture, value system, and climate? The fewer changes the solution requires in the way you are doing business, the smoother its application within the operation will be.

• Your solution strategy should be *divisible*. You should be able to divide the solution strategy into smaller pieces or by location to facilitate ease of implementation. Dividing the strategy should allow you to implement the plan gradually and work out any kinks. This also allows you to build each new step upon the success of previous steps. Avoid all-or-nothing propositions.

• Your solution strategy should be *flexible*. You should be able to alter or adjust as you implement it. Can it be adjusted or otherwise adapted to different situations or requirements? Can you add to it or eliminate part of it? Or is it a "take it or leave it" package? The more flexible your solution is, the happier you ultimately will be with your choice.

• Your solution strategy should be *easily understood*. The solution should be relatively simple and easy to explain to others. Ease of understanding facilitates effective communication, which, in turn, aids implementation attempts.

• Your solution strategy should have realistic *time requirements*. You and others within the organization should have the time required to implement the solution fully and completely without cutting corners or sacrificing quality or quantity. Is the time required for solving your problem consistent with when you need it solved? If you need a change tomorrow, will this solution permit such a rapid change?

• Your solution strategy should fit within your *space requirements*. The strategy should fit your physical plant. If adjustments have to be made, how much will they cost? Is the needed space convenient and accessible? It's better to think about this now rather than later.

• Your solution strategy should take into consideration the amount of *new training* that will be needed. What training or retraining will be necessary to facilitate successful implementation? Do you currently have the training resources, or will additional or outside training resources be needed? Can your people be taught to train others down the line? Is the necessary training minimal, or is it long and involved? Effective training is the key to successful customer service. Consider this criterion carefully. Don't proceed with any solution that fails to meet it.

Training Alternatives

Many of your solution strategies will undoubtedly incorporate revisions and additions to your current training efforts. Consequently, you should consider the following five training alternatives. Each one can play an important role in helping you succeed in your goal of improving the level of service in your operation. The first two training alternatives involve training service personnel. The last three focus on improved ways of training managers.

(1) *Incorporate your quality-service standards and key indicators into training programs for your service personnel.* Job-related training programs are usually developed from a list of tasks or competencies required for that job. So for each service job in the restaurant, you can make a list of required skills, written in the form of "training outcomes"—statements of what the trainee must be able to do by the end of training. Training outcomes for a typical food server might include the ability to take an order, the ability to write food and beverage abbreviations, and the ability to carry several plates without dropping them.

However, if quality service is a goal of a training program, quality-service skills must be included on the list of training outcomes. This means that the ability to provide timely service, to anticipate service needs, to be personally attentive, and to sell by suggestion, as well as

Figure 8-3

Sample Training Outcomes for a Cocktail Server

Traditional Listing	Quality-Service Standards Added
Knowledge Needed:	**Knowledge Needed:**
• Calling order • Price categories and criteria • Abbreviations • Drinks that are poured up or on rocks • Distinction between well, call, and premium • Bar table numbers • I.D. policy • Wine list • Garnishes for drinks	• Thorough knowledge of products in lounge and dining room • Knowledge of restaurant systems that are accommodating to customers
Attitudes Needed:	**Attitudes Needed:**
• Graciousness • Smiling face • Concern for customer • Friendly tone of voice • A good team member	• Smiling body language—entire body, not just the face—reflecting a positive attitude

all the other standards of quality service, must be incorporated into the objectives of training.

Your restaurant's service will begin to improve when the competencies and skills required for quality service are made an integral part of your training system. Figure 8-3 shows a list of common training outcomes for a cocktail server and a listing of quality-service training outcomes that must be added to make the training program a complete one.

Traditional Listing

Skills Needed:

- How to approach a table
- How to take an order
- How to put drinks in calling order
- How to place an order
- How to carry a cocktail tray
- How to check I.D.s
- How to ask for reorders
- How to count out change

Quality-Service Standards Added

Skills Needed:

- Ability to set up an incremental flow of service
- Ability to provide timely service
- Ability to anticipate service needs in advance
- Ability to meet customers' needs as much as possible
- Ability to communicate well
- Ability to obtain feedback from customers
- Ability to be attentive
- Ability to use appropriate and tactful language with customers
- Ability to make helpful suggestions ·
- Ability to sell effectively by suggestion
- Ability to call customers by name
- Ability to be gracious in handling problems or customer complaints

Proficiency levels. After the training outcomes for all service skills have been identified, you should determine the level of proficiency you desire for each service skill. A simple listing of skills or training outcomes is not enough, for it fails to address the question of competency levels.

Take, for example, the skill of filling out a cocktail ticket. Most cocktail servers in restaurants are required to learn this skill. But how is a ticket written? What does a properly filled-out ticket look

Figure 8-4

Sample Training Outcomes and Measurable Proficiency Levels for a Cocktail Server

Selected Traditional Tasks To Be Learned:	Measurable Proficiency Level:
1. Reciting drink prices, drink-price categories, and the criteria for each category	Oral quiz with 100-percent accurate response
2. Greeting a table	a. Giving friendly "hello" b. Obtaining order c. Repeating order d. Saying "thank you"
3. Writing the order on the ticket	a. Using correct abbreviations b. Placing drinks in calling order c. Writing legibly
4. Delivering drinks	a. Giving correct drinks to each customer without having to ask who gets what b. Repeating orders when delivering them c. Asking customers whether they wish to run a tab

like? These questions need to be addressed. We need to know the definition of a "good job" of filling out a cocktail ticket. Before training outcomes can be useful as vehicles of behavioral change, a clear statement of the desired level of proficiency must be made. Cocktail servers, therefore, must not just be trained to put some sort of writing on cocktail tickets. They must be trained to fill out cocktail tickets with all drinks in proper calling order and to use neat writing and correct abbreviations.

Until tickets are written to this standard, the skill cannot be considered mastered. Figure 8-4 shows selected training outcomes for a

Selected Quality-Service Standards To Be Learned:	Measurable Proficiency Level:
1. Anticipation	a. Asking about refills when drinks are one-half to one-quarter full
	b. Asking for help before getting snowed under
2. Timeliness	a. Greeting guests within one minute of their arrival
	b. Delivering drinks within five minutes after they are ordered
3. Communication	a. Giving all customers the correct drink
	b. Informing hostesses of any bar guest who wishes to stay for dinner
	c. Informing manager of any customer who becomes intoxicated
4. Selling Skills	a. Suggesting the house-special drinks
	b. Offering imported beers to beer drinkers

cocktail server and the measurable proficiency levels that might apply to each outcome. If some of them look familiar to you, they should. The key indicators of quality service that you should by now have developed can also serve double-duty as training indicators. They tell you whether a training outcome has been achieved or not.

Be sure to incorporate measurable levels of proficiency for all the service skills into your training system so all service personnel will be trained to the same high level of service expectations. Without a common set of proficiency expectations, the quality of training can vary from one training session to another. The only way to achieve a consistent level of service competency and skill is to define clearly the proficiency level for each service standard, so all trainees and trainers can use them as their standards of excellence.

Changing Behavior

(2) *Use behavioral guidelines and practice sessions as training tools.* If you are going to be effective in training your staff members for quality service, the training programs must affect more than their knowledge and their attitudes; it must also affect their behavior. One key to reinforcing the behavior you want is to provide practice sessions for trainees—before they try their skills in front of real customers.

Most training in food-service operations occurs on the job. Usually tasks are explained, clarified, and then demonstrated. After a (brief) period of observation, most trainees are sent out to wait on customers. Rarely are trainees provided an opportunity to develop their skills in a "safe" or simulated setting until a certain degree of mastery is demonstrated. The absence of this crucial step in the learning process within most restaurants is one of the major weaknesses in food-service training today and helps to account for the widespread inadequacy of service throughout the industry.

One step that can be taken to improve the skills of servers and managers alike is to incorporate time for practice into training programs. Acquiring effective service skills involves the same process as learning how to play tennis, how to count, how to paint a picture, or how to perform brain surgery. All of these require knowledge and practice. We don't put budding musicians on stage to perform without the right background knowledge and plenty of practice. We don't put a tennis player on the tournament court or a brain surgeon in the operating room without having them first demonstrate their knowledge and skill. Why, then, are the great majority of service people in this industry asked to go out and provide service without knowledge and practice in customer-service skills? Effective training requires that time be set aside for skill practice.

Sample Behavioral Guidelines

One way to get the most out of practice sessions is to use behavioral guidelines, or models. A behavioral guideline is simply a "how-to" list for human interaction. The guideline states the criteria for demonstrating a certain behavior. Many training programs are replete with guidelines for performing the technical aspects of the job, but they rarely cover customer relations and service skills.

Using behavioral models as guides, you can set aside time for trainees to gain proficiency in a nonthreatening setting, under the watchful eye of an experienced trainer. This is a powerful training strategy that will work for you. With the behavioral model as a guide, trainees can practice and perfect the attitudes, verbal skills, and body language that translate into effective customer service.

Models can be developed for just about any service skill needed in a restaurant—greeting customers at the front desk or counter, handling a complaining customer, dealing with a difficult customer, or selling by suggestion.

A model for *suggestive selling* might look like the following:

(1) "Read" the guest and decide what to sell.
(2) Expand the customer's awareness of what's available.
(3) Explain the features of what you're selling.
(4) Tell the benefits of what you're selling.
(5) Close the sale.
(6) Compliment the customer's choice.

Here is a sample model for a food server's *greeting a table:*

(1) Greet the party.
(2) Make a positive comment.
(3) Inquire about beverage or cocktail desires before taking the food order.
(4) Provide helpful suggestions if necessary.
(5) Tell what will happen next.

Here is a six-step model for *handling customer complaints:*

(1) Repeat the complaint.
(2) Apologize.
(3) Encourage full disclosure of the problem.
(4) Empathize with the customer's position.
(5) Tell the positive action you will take.
(6) Express appreciation for the feedback.

Behavioral models should be short and sweet, as these three are. A rationale and explanation for each item in the model can be presented when the model is first introduced to the trainees, but the model itself should remain unencumbered by excess words, so it can be readily digested and remembered. Simple explanation may be given aloud or through separate written material. More elaborate explanations may require supplemental material, but the model itself should be kept as simple as possible.

A brief explanation for each of the items in the suggestive-selling model is presented below:

(1) *Read the guest and decide what to sell.* All guests have different needs. Some will be naturals for cocktails, some for wine, some for appetizers, and others for desserts. Tune in to guests' needs. For cues, look at what they've already ordered. Sell an item that complements something they have ordered.

(2) *Expand the customer's awareness of what's available.* Don't assume customers read the menu or table tents. Let them know what's available on and off the menu. Don't ask whether a customer wants an additional item. Suggest one. After all, this is suggestive selling.

(3) *Tell the features of what you're selling.* This is where product knowledge shows. Use it, but avoid unnecessary details. Refer to the senses of taste, smell, and sight. Tell what's unique or different about the product. Describe it with zest.

(4) *Tell the benefits of what you're selling.* Why should the customer buy what you're selling? Value? Quantity? Taste? Offer a good, irresistible reason. There's got to be a benefit.

(5) *Close the sale.* No sale is final until you get the order. Be polite. Help indecisive customers make up their minds. Go for compromises if necessary. One dessert with two forks is better than no dessert order at all.

(6) *Compliment the customer's choice.* Always make customers feel good about their choice.

Trainees should be given the opportunity to practice these and other models in role-playing situations until they can demonstrate the skills comfortably and completely.

Strengthening Supervision Skills of Managers

Management training in most food-service operations centers around technical and administrative skills. New managers learn how to cook, cut meat, control costs, do the books, order food, and so forth. Few of them learn how to interact effectively with a very important group of people—their employees. The problems so many restaurants are having with service can be traced directly to management's inability to supervise employees. This "people" skill can and must be taught. The remaining three training alternatives deal with ways that the supervision skills of restaurant managers can be improved.

Skill Assessments

(1) *Conduct management-skill assessments.* One way to improve your managers' supervisory skills is to build a management-development program around skill assessments. Based on a list of managerial competencies, you can assess the strengths and weaknesses of individual managers. To remedy weak areas, you can generate a specific prescription for supervisory-skill development for each manager (see Figure 8-5).

Individual prescriptions can direct managers to a variety of resources that will assist them in overcoming deficiencies. The resources may include written materials, the boss, a consultant, your state or national restaurant association, a course at a local college or university, or a workshop provided by the training department. The specific mix of resources used depends on the individual manager's weak areas. This type of program works when varied and reliable resources are available, and when the desired competency levels are clearly defined. The success of this type of program also requires careful coordination and tracking of managers' progress. The advantage of an assessment program is that it allows you to create individual development programs for each supervisor.

Contracts

(2) *Conduct management-development workshops with "application contracts."* If you have a group of managers who could benefit

---

Figure 8-5

Management-Skill Assessment Form

Manager _____ Position _____

Date of Assessment _____ Location _____

What does this manager need to improve his or her professional competency?

(1) Knowledge _____
    Action Plan: _____
    Resources to be used: _____
                                               Completion Date

    _____

(2) Skill Training _____
    Action Plan: _____
    Resources to be used: _____
                                               Completion Date

    _____

(3) Management Training _____
    Action Plan: _____
    Resources to be used: _____
                                               Completion Date

    _____

---

from supervisory-skill development, bring them together for a workshop. Have them meet for a few hours one day each week or in a weekend retreat. However the workshops are scheduled, *do* bring your people together to discuss problems and work on improving supervisory skills. Here are just a few of the supervisory skills that could be addressed in these sessions:

> Coaching problem employees
> Communicating effectively
> Delegating effectively
> Diagnosing and solving service problems
> Establishing goals and objectives

Improving interviewing skills
Improving leadership skills
Improving listening skills
Improving training skills
Managing change effectively
Managing time effectively
Motivating employees

These sessions can be run by a management-development expert, but you can also run your own using good resource materials.

The major problem with such workshops is that frequently no effort is made to apply the insights gained from the workshop to specific work situations. The participants may gain tremendous understanding about how to supervise employees more effectively, but all too often these good ideas and techniques are discussed only in the workshops and never leave the room.

This potential problem can be minimized with the use of application contracts. With an application contract, the training doesn't finish until the participants take the information and skills from the workshop and apply them on the job. For example, if a workshop deals with the techniques of management by objectives (MBO), participants are asked to develop a plan for using and practicing the principles of MBO with their employees. They are required to implement this plan and satisfactorily demonstrate the skills they agreed to practice.

Application contracts can be established for any supervisory skill: conducting an interview, terminating an employee, initiating a change, managing time, improving communication, or becoming a better leader. Each application contract should state (1) the desired learning outcomes, (2) an action plan for accomplishing the learning outcomes, and (3) an agreement as to what constitutes satisfactory demonstration of the skill. Skill development is thus incorporated right into the manager's job—the place where it makes a difference.

LCI

(3) *Use learner-controlled instruction for training managers.* Learner-controlled instruction (LCI) is one of the most cost-effective training methods. Instead of employing groups or workshops, LCI

Figure 8-6

Sample Learner-Controlled Training Unit

Competency: Interviewing and Selecting Employees

Final Outcome: At the completion of this unit, you will be able to conduct an interview session with a prospective employee according to the guidelines of proper interviewing, make a reference check, and make a hire/do-not-hire decision based on the information obtained.

Strategies for Developing Competency	Proficiency Standard
(1) Read "Manager-Training Packet #10" on interviewing and selecting employees.	You read the training information packet and answer the questions at the end of the packet.
(2) Observe your training manager interviewing a job applicant.	You are able to explain the stages of an interview and the techniques used by the interviewer.
	You are able to rate how the interview was conducted according to the guidelines in training packet #10.

takes place on the job. It can be implemented both in small companies and large ones with widely scattered units. LCI puts the responsibility for the development of skills on the trainees themselves. They control when a skill is mastered and, in many cases, how it is developed.

How does an LCI program work? Trainees are given a list of competencies that they are responsible for learning. The method of measuring the extent of competency in each skill is included in this list, along with resources and suggested strategies for developing the skill. With that, managers are on their own to develop the skills. When they can demonstrate the required level of proficiency, a mentor, boss, or training supervisor verifies the trainee's mastery of the skill.

(3) You conduct an interview with a job applicant, with your training manager participating.	At the end of the interview, you can evaluate accurately how closely you followed the guidelines in training packet #10.
	You can identify the area(s) where you need to improve your interview technique.
(4) Repeat step #3, as needed.	You can comfortably meet the interviewing guidelines during an interview.
(5) Make a reference check for a possible hire.	You reach the previous employer and obtain information about the applicant.
(6) You make a hiring decision.	The new employee successfully completes the training and probationary periods.

Resources Available: Manager-Training Packet #10
Your Training Manager
Your Divisional Manager

Verification of Completion:
Date of Completion _____
Training Manager's Signature _____

The program is completed when the trainee demonstrates competency in all the skills in the program.

A sample LCI learning unit for one skill, interviewing and selecting employees, is shown in Figure 8-6. A complete LCI program consists of learning units similar to this for all of the skills a person must master to be an excellent manager.

An additional benefit of LCI programs is that while they are an effective way to strengthen supervisory skills, the process required for successful completion of such a program develops other important skills as well. By successfully completing an LCI program, managers have demonstrated the abilities of self-discipline, self-motivation, self-direction, and self-organization. Each of these abilities is a vital skill for restaurant managers. Yet they won't necessarily learn these skills unless the management-training program provides the opportunity.

In Summary

I have suggested a number of helpful tools in this chapter that can be used to develop effective service-improvement strategies. A force-field analysis will help you uncover all the forces currently helping or hindering your efforts to improve customer service. Generating a variety of alternative solution strategies opens the field of options so that the best possible solution for your specific situation can be chosen. Effective training-improvement strategies require that you make quality-service standards an integral part of your training programs. Making use of service-behavior models and practice sessions also goes a long way toward improving service skills in employees.

Another effective way of improving employees' service abilities is to nurture strong supervisory skills among your managers by using individual skill assessments, group workshops, or learner-controlled instruction formats. Regardless of how you go about developing your managers' supervisory skills, this training is time and money well invested, because effective supervisory training leads directly to improved service in the dining room.

With these tools and ideas in hand, you should now have a set of strategies in mind that you can implement in your restaurant. But you must be judicious in your implementation of these strategies. You may have the best solution strategies in the world, but if you fail to pay attention to a few simple rules of strategy implementation, your well-laid plans may meet with mediocre success or even total disaster. In the next chapter, I will discuss how to get your plans successfully off the ground.

Initiating Your Service-Improvement Strategies

9

THE GROUNDWORK for implementing your service-improvement strategies is completed. Now it is time to transform your plans into action.

Your first step is to consider the optimum means of implementing your plans. Well-intentioned owners, operators, and managers too often grab hold of a given strategy for improving their operation without stopping to figure out the best way to proceed. They may overlook the fact that when new ideas, policies, and procedures are introduced into an operation, there is a high probability of at least some resistance. The resistance may come from individuals or certain organizational characteristics that may interfere with the plans. Resistance may result from the way the strategy is introduced or because of the person who introduced it. Failure to understand and deal with potential resistance to your efforts may lead to the ultimate failure of your plans to put quality into your food service, no matter how good those plans might be.

I consider this point so important that I am devoting this entire chapter to a discussion of how you should implement your service-improvement strategies. I will explain where resistance to your efforts to change service behaviors will come from and what you can constructively do to reduce this resistance. I emphasize the importance of involving your service personnel and managers in the implementation process, the necessity of effectively communicating what it is that you want to accomplish, and the importance of remaining open and flexible during this entire process. This chapter will help you get your ideas and plans going successfully.

The Roots of Potential Resistance

Just because *you* want to make a change in the service behavior of your managers and service personnel, don't assume that *they* want to make a change. In fact, your staff may be quite content with the way things are right now. Moreover, change usually generates a defensive or resistant reaction in many people.

What causes this resistance? Why won't everybody see the need for change as you do? The answers to these questions can be found in the psychological framework of most people, as well as in the way work groups are organized. These "roots of resistance" are ever-present. They can emerge any time someone attempts to make changes within an organization. The difference between a successful change and an unsuccessful one often lies in how the roots of resistance are dealt with. Let's first see what these roots of resistance are and then discuss how best to deal with them.

Root of Resistance #1: *Differing perceptions.* We view the world and what happens in it through our own unique set of lenses. Our individual lenses have been molded by our previous experiences and established value systems, as well as our entire psychological make-up. We all see things differently, and we also remember things differently. We perceive and remember selectively. We are sensitive to certain stimuli and insensitive to others. In your restaurant, therefore, your managers may not see the service situation exactly as you see it, and the service personnel may see it in yet another way. Moreover, various members of your service staff will perceive the level of service in diverse ways. Every individual on your service team has a unique framework through which he or she interprets the world. Other people may resist your attempts at change simply because they see the problem differently from you. They may not see any problem at all! They may not see service as a priority, or they may view your suggestions as inappropriate and misguided. Your failure to consider these differing perceptions will create resistance to your ideas and proposals.

Root of Resistance #2: *Old habits.* Habits cause us to resist new ways of doing things. When we engage in the same activity over and over again, we soon develop our own comfortable way of doing it.

Whether it is getting dressed, washing the dishes, or serving customers, we generally develop predictable ways of behaving. These habits can be a source of stability and continuity, but they also mold behavior so profoundly that it can be quite difficult to make changes.

In restaurants, many service behaviors that grow into habits are implanted during the early days of training. These early experiences are critical, for these first successes at mastering a difficult task or skill usually have a lasting impact on us. As a result, many managers and service personnel have no real desire to change their service habits. They are quite comfortable performing their jobs the way they were originally taught—the way they have always done it—whether they are meeting current job expectations or not. Behavior that has become a habit usually continues in the same way until something significant alters it.

Root of Resistance #3: *Personal weaknesses.* Some persons' resistance to new ideas and ways of doing things is due to their feeling that they have no power to change. This feeling of impotence is supported by the perception that "others," usually bosses or customers, are the reason for the current state of affairs. These individuals see themselves as helpless victims of circumstances, and they see others as being responsible for their behavior. When asked to change their behavior, these employees respond: "You need to change *them* first."

Self-distrust is a spinoff of feelings of impotence. Individuals who distrust themselves will resist what you are trying to do because they don't believe they can do what you ask. They don't trust their own ability to become a better sales representative, to become more attentive to customers' needs, or to improve service. And since they are unable to change their behavior, they continue with what they have been doing all along.

Other individuals will resist your attempts to improve service skills out of insecurity, which is a cause of anxiety. New ways of doing things threaten people who find security and comfort in the tried and true. These people avoid change and seek standards and systems that have served the test of time. To them, change introduces the unknown and the threat of losing something. Often these people are not quite sure what it is that they are going to lose, but whatever it is, they don't want to lose it. Add personal insecurity to feelings of impotence and self-distrust, and you will find a winning combination for resisting almost every new idea and suggestion that comes along.

Root of Resistance #4: *Previous behavioral expectations*. Every workplace operates on an established set of norms. Norms reflect the rules of acceptable and unacceptable behavior for members of the organization. Norms provide the operational "glue" for groups. And since norms are shared, group members adjust their behavior to the expectations of the group to which they belong. In a way, group membership is defined by those willing to abide by the norms of the group. Group pressures reinforce and perpetuate expected patterns of behavior. Norms become ingrained in a group's way of doing things, and change is made more difficult.

When you attempt to change the service behavior of your managers and service personnel, you are challenging existing group norms. In essence, you are proposing a new set of norms to replace a previous set. Approach tampering with existing norms carefully. When the group perceives that something they hold dear is under attack, their response may carry a high emotional charge.

Root of Resistance #5: *Interests under attack*. An attack on vested interests usually prompts resistance to change. Usually these interests involve money, power, and status. When any one or any combination of the three are threatened, the consequences will be resistance to change. The threats against vested interests don't even have to be real. Imagined threats can draw as much resistance as genuine ones.

If members of your service staff feel, for example, that your proposals jeopardize their pocketbook, you've got a fight on your hands. Some food servers (e.g., those working in a "factory-style" operation) might resist adopting more convivial mannerisms for fear that the number of table turns will be reduced, and their opportunity to receive tips will be cut.

You will also meet resistance if your plan threatens the status of any one group in your operation. One service crew known for its unique outfits resisted their boss's choice of new uniforms. The crew members perceived the new outfits as failing to set them apart from other food servers. The new attire destroyed the unique, special feeling they had about themselves. Within three months, the restaurant restored the original uniforms.

Responding to Resistance: Four Basic Foundations

To offset or eliminate the resistance that you may encounter in your efforts to implement your solution strategies and improve customer service in your operation, you should build on the four basic foundations of change management. These foundations are (1) **sharing information with your people,** (2) **involving your employees,** (3) **implementing your solution strategies in increments,** and (4) **remaining flexible.** I will explain each one in detail.

Foundation #1: *Sharing information.* Give your crew all the information you can about what you want to do and why. Hold information-sharing meetings. Make as many personal contacts as you can. Your purpose here is to gain the staff's support for your solution strategies. So let managers and employees know the overall benefits of your proposal and how they will personally gain from it. Emphasize how your proposal is consistent with the existing organizational values and how it will help organizational objectives. Appeal to employees' sense of interest and excitement. Your program will be a new experience—so generate enthusiasm for it.

As you "talk up" your project, some employees will raise valid objections. Listen to them carefully. Avoid being locked into a definitive solution at this point. Be willing to make some adjustments to improve the plan or make it more acceptable to the staff. Above all, relieve any fears or anxieties employees may voice. Inevitably some of the information that you share will be misunderstood and misinterpreted. In such cases, provide plenty of opportunities for feedback and clarification. Make sure that any and all misunderstandings and misinterpretations are corrected. Effective communication is the first step toward getting your solution strategies for improving service successfully off the ground.

Foundation #2: *Employee involvement.* Involve your managers and service personnel as much as possible in the implementation process so that your people feel that they are "in on things." Involvement also works to get the attitudes of your employees on your side, because employees gain "ownership" of the project. When your people have a hand in molding and constructing service-improvement strategies, they will perceive proposed ideas for changing service behavior as their own. Moreover, your employees may make useful suggestions for improving your solution strategies. Promote and encourage their input. You will find that your managers and service people have many fine ideas for improving service.

If you have involved your managers and service personnel in the diagnostic efforts suggested in Chapter 7, you have set the stage for employee participation and collaboration. Failure to continue that collaborative effort at this stage could be disastrous.

Foundation #3: *Incremental implementation.* A common trap for many advocates of change is biting off more than the organization can chew at any one time. Change is easily digested when it is divided into palatable pieces. You're not going to alter everyone's service behavior in one meeting. Don't even try this "shotgun" approach. Spend your energy more constructively by setting up a realistic plan of attack. Move gradually by working first with one major problem in one service group. Focus your attention where it is needed most— on the group that needs the most improvement. Use this pilot to straighten out any kinks in your strategies. Establish a foundation of success and then move on.

If yours is a multiunit organization, work with one or two restaurants in a pilot program before tackling major organizational changes. As you go along, find out what works and what doesn't. Build on a reputation of success rather than one of failure. When you are comfortable that your efforts are working, expand your step-by-step timetable for implementation. Above all, keep your expectations realistic. The more significant the changes you are trying to make, the longer it will take to gain their acceptance and adoption throughout your operation.

Foundation #4: *Flexibility.* If you approach the improvement of your operation with a rigid plan of attack, you will most likely have a great deal of trouble getting off square one. Your chances of succeeding will be enhanced by adapting and readapting solution strategies throughout the implementation process. Being flexible may even mean that ultimately you must change your implementation plans altogether.

Even when you have done a very careful job of selecting and adjusting your service-improvement strategies to your own operation, you may still find that more adaptation is necessary. You should be prepared to make concessions to meet the legitimate objections of managers or employees. Avoid sacrificing your long-term successes to gain a few momentary victories along the way. Keep your sights on your overall objectives, always reminding yourself that major change comes slowly.

Sometimes you can overanticipate resistance or complications, and develop an overly elaborate plan for proceeding. If you find this is the case, accelerate the pace of implementation. Simplify your plan and get on with it.

On the other hand, the staff's resistance may be more than you bargained for. Perhaps your employees need to absorb more information, or they need more time for discussion, planning, or trial runs. Under these circumstances, you should slow down. This doesn't mean give up; it merely means shifting gears to provide for a more realistic pace of implementation.

Throughout this book I have urged you to be open and collaborate with your managers and service personnel. While this approach is more likely than any other to ensure the success of your service-improvement strategies, sometimes collaboration just doesn't work.

When collaboration fails, you may have to implement change from your position of power in the organization. If earnest and skillful efforts to reduce resistance have been fruitless, and you (the person bearing ultimate responsibility) believe that certain actions are necessary to improve customer service, you should make these changes from your rightful position of authority. Operating from a position of power remains your "ace in the hole," but it is also your last trump. Refrain from using it until you absolutely have to, but be flexible enough to use it when necessary.

The Ten Steps to Successful Implementation

The major principles reflected in the four foundations of successful change management can be translated into ten specific steps that lead to successful implementation of new ideas and ways of doing things. If you follow each of these steps (which summarize the previous points), your effectiveness in improving the service skills of your managers and service people will be at the maximum.

(1) Allow your managers and service people to join in the diagnosis of the basic service problems.
(2) Involve managers and service personnel so that they feel the changes are their own.
(3) Develop solutions that reduce present job burdens.
(4) Produce solutions that are consistent with the values and ideals that have long been acknowledged by the organization.
(5) Generate changes that offer the kind of new experiences that will excite your service crew and management team.
(6) Avoid threatening the autonomy and security of your managers and service people.
(7) Recognize that valid objections will emerge. Be responsive to these objections and empathize with resistors.
(8) Provide plenty of feedback and clarification to dispel any misunderstandings and misinterpretations that may develop.
(9) Keep your solution strategies open to revision and reconsideration if experience indicates that changes would be desirable.
(10) Promote acceptance, support, and trust among your managers and service personnel throughout the entire organization.

After Implementation, What?

So you've been flexible, adaptable, communicative, involving, and supportive. Your solution strategies are successfully implemented, and they are well accepted. Service behavior is showing definite improvement. Things are looking good—in fact, better than you ever expected. The service you are providing is moving from "run o' the mill" to "top of the crop."

Now how are you going to keep service running at this quality level? How can you convert the changes that you have just successfully implemented into standard operating procedures? How can you help guarantee that future managers and service personnel will carry on with the tradition that you have so successfully started? I will answer these questions in the next chapter.

Strengthening Quality Service Through Feedback, Recognition, and Rewards

10

THE CHANGES in service behavior that you have successfully brought about may end up producing only short-term results, unless you ensure their permanence with long-term reinforcement—feedback, recognition, and rewards. Once you have identified and defined competencies, and your staff is trained, these skills must be woven into the very fabric of the operation. Continuous performance feedback for all managers and service personnel is a major thread in this fabric. So is giving rewards and recognition for satisfactory demonstration of competency in service skills. You must make it personally advantageous for managers and service personnel alike to provide quality service to customers.

The Importance of Feedback

Lack of feedback eventually leads to the extinction of the behavior that you desire. Even though specific competencies have been identified and included in training programs, quality service will not survive without a continuous system of feedback to the people responsible for providing service.

The game of bowling clearly shows the importance of feedback. One likely reason for bowling's popularity is that players receive immediate feedback on how well they are doing. All they have to do is count the number of pins left standing after each ball. Imagine bowling with a curtain shielding your view of the pins. You roll the ball under the curtain, and you hear some pins fall. You don't know how many fell, and nobody tells you. Few people would continue to enjoy bowling under those circumstances. Yet we expect the people who work for us to do their jobs each day without receiving regular feedback on how they are doing. It's a wonder they keep it up as long as they do. Performance on a job, like bowling, requires feedback. Service employees need to have information "fed back" to them on their level of performance.

The Importance of Positive Reinforcement

The feedback and reward ideas suggested in this chapter are based on the psychological concept of "positive reinforcement." According to the theory of reinforcement, all behavior is a function of its consequences. Positive consequences tend to strengthen a given action and encourage its repetition. On the other hand, when a behavior is followed by no consequences or by negative consequences, the frequency of that behavior usually diminishes.

Focusing on positive reinforcement directs your attention and the attention of your managers and service people to the behavior you want—not the behavior you don't want. This helps maintain a positive sense of direction and focus. In such an atmosphere, catching somebody doing something right becomes much more important than catching them doing something wrong.

In restaurants, positive reinforcement all too frequently plays second string to negative reinforcement and punishment as a means of influencing behavior. Applying negative consequences will reduce the frequency of undesirable behaviors over the short term, but frequent application of negative consequences eventually creates more problems than it solves. A work atmosphere overloaded with negative reinforcement and punishment generates antagonism and distrust and cripples productivity. Employees become aggressive and disruptive—even working to sabotage the very results you desire.

Quality service in restaurants cannot be developed in an atmosphere of apprehension and fear. As I have said before, it must grow out of respect and trust. You must create an atmosphere in which managers and crew members can work together toward the same goals. You can do this with effective use of positive reinforcement through recognition and rewards.

There are three simple ways to provide feedback to your managers and service personnel about their service behavior: (1) conduct regular performance appraisals based on quality-service standards, (2) record and chart sales performance, and (3) promote and encourage meaningful customer feedback. I will suggest several examples of how you can do each of these three things.

Performance Appraisals. Commendable job performance should be verbally recognized each day. Beyond this, more formal performance appraisals should be conducted with managers and service personnel on a regular three- to six-month schedule. These sessions should be conducted in a nonthreatening environment with an emphasis on specific, demonstrated behavior. Put your stress on what the employee is doing right. Identify areas needing improvement and reach an agreement on a strategy or plan of action for improving each weak performance area. The performance-appraisal session should conclude with the mutual establishment of performance objectives for the employee and specific schedules for feedback and accomplishment of the objectives.

The criteria for evaluating performance should be based on demonstrated behavior, not personality characteristics. Identified quality-service standards and their indicators can easily be adapted into performance-appraisal criteria (as shown in Figure 10-1). Notice that this evaluation form for a host or hostess incorporates both convivial and procedural service skills. The form provides for the evaluation of a person's performance in the critical skill areas demanded by the job. All skills are specifically spelled out. An evaluation form of this type leaves little question as to what kind of behavior is required in the job.

Similar evaluation forms should be developed for all the service and management functions in your food-service operation. Each of these evaluation instruments should constitute a review of all the skill competencies required in the job. Technical, supervisory, procedural, and convivial skills must all be addressed. If you want feedback to reinforce the behavior appropriate to the job, including quality-service behavior, the form that you use to provide this feedback must also completely reflect all of the skills and standards that define success for that job.

Figure 10-1

Sample Host or Hostess Evaluation Form

Name of Employee _____ Date _____

Rater's Name _____ Title _____

Job Competency: Customer-Relations Skills

Job Competency: Customer-Relations Skills	Always	Mostly	Some-times	Rarely	Never
1. This person demonstrates the ability to answer correctly common questions asked by customers.	5	4	3	2	1
2. This person greets customers with a friendly welcome and big smile.	5	4	3	2	1
3. This person talks with customers as they are escorted to their seats.	5	4	3	2	1
4. This person wishes a warm "good night" to departing guests.	5	4	3	2	1
5. This person asks for guest feedback from departing guests.	5	4	3	2	1
6. This person makes eye contact when talking with customers.	5	4	3	2	1
7. This person handles customer complaints graciously and politely.	5	4	3	2	1
8. This person acknowledges waiting customers immediately upon their arrival, even when busy.	5	4	3	2	1
9. This person refers to customers by name.	5	4	3	2	1

	Always	Mostly	Some-times	Rarely	Never
10. This person calls customers by name when addressing them.	5	4	3	2	1
11. This person tries hard to meet reasonable customer requests.	5	4	3	2	1
12. This person acknowledges special needs of customers for highchairs, booster seats, room for wheelchairs, etc.	5	4	3	2	1
13. This person shows customers enthusiasm toward the job.	5	4	3	2	1
14. This person is able to make menu recommendations upon customer inquiry.	5	4	3	2	1

Comments about customer-relations skills: _____

Job Competency: Seating Skills

	Always	Mostly	Some-times	Rarely	Never
15. This person records the correct table number on the ticket when seating guests.	5	4	3	2	1
16. This person walks at the pace of the customers when escorting them to their tables.	5	4	3	2	1
17. This person waits at the table until all guests are seated.	5	4	3	2	1
18. This person makes ordering suggestions when handing menus out to guests.	5	4	3	2	1

Figure 10-1 (continued)
Sample Host or Hostess Evaluation Form

	Always	Mostly	Some-times	Rarely	Never
19. This person quotes accurate waiting times when there is a wait to be seated.	5	4	3	2	1
20. This person avoids using the P.A. system, when possible, to inform waiting customers that their tables are ready.	5	4	3	2	1
21. This person helps control the flow by seating customers evenly through the sections and at staggered times, if possible.	5	4	3	2	1
22. This person communicates seating and other needs effectively to other service personnel.	5	4	3	2	1
23. This person performs the seating function in an organized way.	5	4	3	2	1

Comments about seating skills: _____

Job Competency: Telephone Skills

	Always	Mostly	Some-times	Rarely	Never
24. This person answers the phone in a friendly and helpful tone of voice.	5	4	3	2	1
25. This person answers the phone with, "Hello, thank you for calling the Top of the Crop. This is (name). How can I help you?"	5	4	3	2	1
26. This person avoids accepting personal phone calls.	5	4	3	2	1

	Always	Mostly	Some-times	Rarely	Never
27. This person projects a positive telephone personality.	5	4	3	2	1

Comments about telephone skills: _____

Job Competency: Proper Image

	Always	Mostly	Sometimes	Rarely	Never
28. This person's attire is clean and neat.	5	4	3	2	1
29. This person dresses properly for the position.	5	4	3	2	1
30. This person keeps a neat and tidy front desk.	5	4	3	2	1
31. This person avoids combing hair or applying makeup while stationed at the front desk.	5	4	3	2	1
32. This person never sits down or reads at the station.	5	4	3	2	1
33. This person avoids chewing gum and smoking at the station.	5	4	3	2	1

Comments on image: _____

34. List and describe any job accomplishments and strengths that have not been noted earlier.

35. List and describe any areas requiring improvement.

Signature of Rater _____ Signature of Employee _____
Date _____ Date _____

The criteria used to evaluate job performance in your operation should parallel those competencies and skills taught in your training programs. If you appraise the skills that are trained and train employees in the skills that are appraised, you can develop a strong, synergistic mechanism to help your managers and staff master the service behavior you want. When training and feedback systems work to reinforce and support each other, both become more effective in producing the behavior desired in managers and service employees.

Recording Sales Performance. It is amazing how few restaurants record or chart the sales efforts of each individual sales representative. This practice, which is taken for granted in such other sales-oriented concerns as automobile, clothing, insurance, and real-estate companies, is rarely used in restaurants to promote or reward food and beverage sales efforts.

If order takers are going to be converted into effective sellers, you must give them feedback regarding their sales performance. These individual sales-performance records should be made available to the whole staff. Every seller should know what all the other sellers are producing, and they should have the opportunity to compare results with one another. Like a bowling score, sales figures speak for themselves. A restaurant can increase sales dramatically just by posting individual sales efforts. So establish some realistic sales goals, supply some feedback, and watch your service personnel become effective sellers.

You can record daily food and beverage totals for each server on a chart like the one in Figure 10-2. This chart shows a breakdown of food, dessert, and bar sales. Your breakdown, of course, may vary according to the specific needs and data desired for your operation. It is important to note, however, that on this chart total sales are divided by the number of hours worked to show the productivity measure of sales per hour. If sales per hour are not calculated, the total sales figure for each individual for a given day may be deceiving. Although Mary Smith has logged more sales than any other server in the example, her productivity, measured in average sales per hour, is lower than that of two other employees. When your service people work varying numbers of hours for any given day, dividing total sales for the day by the number of hours worked reflects a realistic pro-

Figure 10-2

Sample Daily Sales Report

Day _____ Date _____

Server's Name	Food	Dessert	Bar	TOTAL SALES	Hours Worked	PRODUCTIVITY Sales/Hour
Mary Smith	$200	$10	$190	$400	10	$40
Bob Jones	175	20	25	220	4	55
Alice Johnson	50	25	150	225	3	75
Bill Hamilton	220	10	10	240	8	30
JoAnn Hodge			210	210	6	35

ductivity figure for each individual. (You can also use other measures, such as covers per hour.)

A graphic display of a week's worth of sales figures (like the one in Figure 10-3) shows at a glance who are the best and the weakest sales people.

Fluctuations in productivity may occur, of course, depending on the time or the shift that each person works. To compensate for this, separate charts can be kept for the different shifts, or a shift notation can be made on the weekly productivity chart itself.

Weekly trends in average sales for each server can also be graphed. Sales figures can be categorized according to your needs. The chart in the example (Figure 10–4) shows a breakdown for wine sales, liquor sales, and food sales. It also graphs the overall sales per head from week to week.

The "goal line" is an important part of this chart. The presence of a specific goal gives a common direction toward which all service personnel can strive. A chart such as this provides a vivid display of how the service crew is doing from week to week, and it gives them a goal to reach and sustain.

Figure 10-3

Sample Weekly Productivity Chart

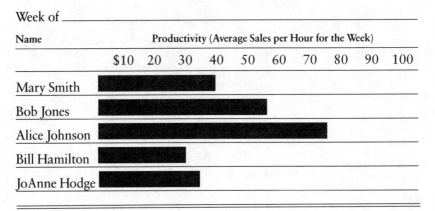

Week of _____

Name	Productivity (Average Sales per Hour for the Week)									
	$10	20	30	40	50	60	70	80	90	100
Mary Smith										
Bob Jones										
Alice Johnson										
Bill Hamilton										
JoAnne Hodge										

Encouraging Customer Feedback. As I stated at the beginning of this book, restaurant customers play a significant role in the perpetuation of poor service in restaurants because of their tipping behavior. Tips fail to reinforce quality service because too many customers leave them for reasons unrelated to the quality of the service rendered. But even if customers *did* tip according to the level of service they received, without verbal feedback the server hasn't a clue as to why customers left the amount they did.

The tradition of tipping has come a long way from its beginnings in England over 200 years ago. Samuel Johnson is given credit for starting the tradition that has grown into the present-day tip. In the London coffeehouses of the 18th Century, Johnson and his friends would hand their server a slip of paper with coins attached. On the paper was written, "To Insure Promptness." The acronym of this phrase is apparently the derivation of the word "tip."[8]

Unfortunately, the tradition of tipping grew from providing encouragement for quality service beforehand, to one that is *expected*

---

[8]Tippers International, *Guide for Tipping* (Oshkosh, WI: Tippers International).

Figure 10-4

Sample Average-Sales-per-Head Chart

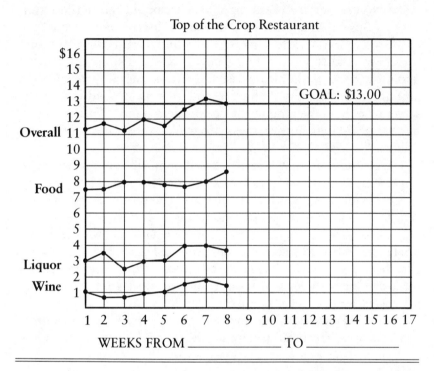

Top of the Crop Restaurant

WEEKS FROM _____ TO _____

regardless of the quality of service rendered. The tradition of the un-earned tip is alive and well today. If restaurant customers would ac-tually tip according to the level of service received, the tip could be-come a powerful reinforcement for quality service.

Restaurant customers often say that they tip according to the level of service received, but research shows this is not the case. A study on tipping behavior found that most diners tip from 12 to 17 percent, regardless of the level of service they received. The researchers found that one factor affecting the level of tipping was the method of pay-ment. When payment was made by credit card, tips averaged over one percentage point higher than with cash payment. Another factor was group size; parties of one or two tipped more than larger groups. The third significant factor was the physical appearance of the food server. Attractive waitresses received significantly higher tips than less-attractive waitresses. In fact, attractive servers who provided poor service received higher tips than less-attractive servers who provided excellent service.[9] With tipping behavior like this, it is no wonder that tips fail to reinforce the level of service customers want.

Customer feedback to servers. Tips could serve as powerful reinforcers of quality service if customers could (1) know the criteria upon which the tip should be based, (2) use an easy way to figure the amount of tip that should be left, and (3) provide feedback to the server as to how the amount of tip was determined. The customer-feedback card in Figure 10-5 was designed to satisfy these three conditions.

The customer-feedback card is based on the idea of positive reinforcement. The card outlines five basic actions expected from service. The behavior demonstrated by the server can produce a tip of from zero to 15 percent or more, depending on the rating received in each of the five categories. The better the service rendered, the higher the tip. Furthermore, by reviewing the completed card, the server knows exactly which behavior has been rewarded. Because servers are not rewarded for behavior that is not exhibited, the form tells them exactly what behavior needs improvement.

Use of this form does not limit a tip to 15 percent. Extraordinary service can be rewarded to any degree deemed appropriate by the customer, if the level of service goes beyond the criteria listed on the card.

Customer feedback to managers. Managers also can benefit from clear and concise feedback from customers. The more aware managers are of the level of service customers are receiving, the more they can reward the behavior they desire and take appropriate actions when the behavior is less than desirable. The customer-feedback card for managers (see Figure 10-6) provides an opportunity for customers to tell managers how well the service they received measured up to their expectations.

---

[9]Joanne M. May, "Looking for Tips: An Empirical Perspective on Restaurant Tipping," *The Cornell Hotel and Restaurant Administration Quarterly,* 20, No. 4 (February 1980), pp. 6-13.

Figure 10-5

Customer-Feedback Card

To the server: This card has been designed to reinforce and reward the level of service I want as a restaurant customer. Your tip has been based on the percentages circled for each of the five standards of quality service below.

AS A SERVER, YOU WERE

	NO			YES
1. Timely	0%	1%	2%	3%
2. Flexible	0%	1%	2%	3%
3. Attentive	0%	1%	2%	3%
4. Friendly	0%	1%	2%	3%
5. Helpful	0%	1%	2%	3%
6. Other:				____%

Total tip _____ % of bill

Figure 10-6

Customer-Feedback Card for Managers

To the manager: This card has been designed to reinforce and reward the type of service that I want as a restaurant customer, and to give you feedback on the training and supervision of your service personnel.

THE SERVICE THAT I RECEIVED WAS

	NO			YES
1. Timely	0	1	2	3
2. Flexible	0	1	2	3
3. Attentive	0	1	2	3
4. Friendly	0	1	2	3
5. Helpful	0	1	2	3
6. Other _____	0	1	2	3

Overall, I found service to be *Excellent* (15 or above); *Good* (14–12); *Fair* (11–9); *Poor* (8 or below).

This form makes it easy for customers to evaluate the level of service they receive. It also supplies specific feedback to the manager regarding which behavior is being exhibited on the dining-room floor and which is not.

Recognition and Rewards

In addition to providing feedback to managers and service personnel about their service ability, you can permanently shift service levels by allowing your staff members to benefit personally when they demonstrate the level of performance you ask. You can do this by providing appropriate recognition and rewards to reinforce desirable service behaviors.

Rewarding a given behavior increases the repetition of that behavior, and proper forms of recognition and rewards help nurture a sense of pride and accomplishment in your employees. Used correctly, recognition and rewards will build a genuine commitment among your managers and service people to improving service behaviors, and also to you and the organization.

Incentives vs. benefits. Recognition and rewards are forms of incentives. So is additional compensation for employees for behaving in desirable ways. Incentives should not be confused with benefits, however. Everybody in the organization receives benefits merely for being an employee. Each employee receives a regular paycheck, for instance, and many receive health insurance and meal privileges. Benefits are nondiscriminatory; everybody receives them, regardless of their performance. Incentives, on the other hand, are granted when certain predetermined and specific actions or performance levels are achieved. Incentives are tied to performance; benefits are not.

Criteria for effective incentives. To be effective, incentives must not only be given in a discriminating fashion, but their distribution must also be based on clear and concise criteria that are announced in advance. Employees must meet certain requirements or standards before they become eligible to receive an incentive.

A common incentive is an "Employee of the Month" program. But such recognition will do little to promote and encourage employees to act in specific ways if the criteria upon which a choice is made are vague, unknown, or nonexistent. (Announcing why Mary Smith, for example, was selected as "Employee of the Month" after the selection was made fails to give all employees the same opportunity to attain the desired goal.) If, on the other hand, the criteria for choosing an employee of the month are clearly specified, so everybody in the organization understands how and why people are chosen, more employees will direct their actions toward that specific behavior.

When incentives are given to employees on a discriminating basis, when they are based on clear and concise criteria, and when these criteria are established and announced in advance, the incentive program can work significantly toward shaping and reinforcing quality service.

Behavior reinforcement through recognition and rewards comes in two varieties: (1) frequent informal reinforcement, and (2) intermittent formal reinforcement.

Frequent informal reinforcement. No reinforcement is more effective than a genuine acknowledgement of a job well done. The dramatic power of verbal praise lies not only in the value of feedback itself, but also in our psychological need to have our efforts recognized. When we receive praise, we know that our work efforts have been noticed. This increases our self-esteem, gives us pride, and makes us feel part of the team. These feelings, in turn, control our will to perform. We all want to perform well when we are given credit that has been rightfully earned. Praise given when it is due is one of the strongest motivators available.

When management praise is not forthcoming, subordinates soon begin to feel unappreciated, insignificant, or out of touch with the organization. No manager should ever be too busy, too preoccupied, or too insensitive to the needs of employees to praise them frequently for jobs well done. Understandably, it is far easier to sit here and read about the necessity of praising your employees than it is to go out and praise them each day. Simply telling others how well they are doing somehow falls through the cracks, or gets lost in the press of getting other things done. Yet in the final analysis, things tend not to get done right without such praise.

As with other forms of feedback, praise should be as specific as possible. Instead of merely saying, "Good job tonight, Frank," you should zero in on exactly what made it a good night for Frank. Maybe it was the number of specials he sold. Perhaps it was how he handled a difficult customer, or maybe it was how he kept control during a very hectic period. Whatever it was, focus your comments on the exact reason for the praise.

The more specific you are, the more effective you will be in directing behavior. This requires that your "radar" be continually tuned in to what is going on around you—and that you be aware of how your employees are behaving in front of customers. Look for your service indicators, because they will help you be specific.

Intermittent rewards and recognition. The intervals of intermittent positive reinforcement can be as brief as a week or as long as a quarter. The right interval for your operation will depend on your specific needs and organizational characteristics. As with frequent praise, intermittent reinforcement must be tied to specific, clear, and concise behavioral expectations that are announced in advance. Intermittent rewards must be discriminating, so that only individuals demonstrating the expected behavior receive them. Otherwise, the rewards that you give will fail to guide behavior effectively.

Intermittent positive reinforcement is usually more formal than one-on-one verbal praise, because the former is often made public within the organization (and sometimes outside the organization). Special recognition at staff meetings, publicity in a company newsletter or in the local press, and a plaque or photograph placed in a strategic location are ways often used to announce an award for exemplary service.

This type of reinforcement usually involves a specific reward. Two dozen examples follow:

(1) Offer a cash percentage for each special or earmarked item sold.
(2) Provide a given cash amount for selling the most of a specified item.
(3) Give a percentage bonus based on volume of sales.
(4) Give a group bonus for meeting a specified group goal.
(5) Provide for group profit-sharing upon meeting a specified goal.
(6) Give a bottle of wine for the most wine sales on one night.
(7) Provide a paid trip to a wine seminar for the highest wine sales.
(8) Offer complimentary cocktails for highest cocktail sales during an evening.

(9) Pay for a weekend for two at a local resort.

(10) Offer a complimentary meal for two.

(11) Recognize special contributions through an employee of the month, quarter, etc., program.

(12) Give tickets to a sporting event or a musical.

(13) Schedule paid time off.

(14) Give gift certificates to a local store.

(15) Offer complimentary T-shirts.

(16) Throw a group party or cookout.

(17) Obtain individual recognition in the news media.

(18) Engrave the names of outstanding performers on a plaque.

(19) Provide special parking privileges.

(20) Grant pay increases.

(21) Organize a group outing or special event.

(22) Hand out special recognition pins.

(23) Provide choice of work schedule.

(24) Write a letter of recognition from the highest level of management.

Is This All?

Proper feedback, recognition, and rewards will work to keep your service on the right track. They will help motivate your managers and service people alike to move in the direction you desire. Without feedback, recognition, and rewards, any improvement you achieve in the level of customer service in your operation will slowly regress until your employees are back to their previous levels of performance. Your long-term prospects for permanently instilling quality-service behavior as part and parcel of your organization lie in the effective use of feedback, recognition, and rewards.

As the drawing in Figure 10-7 illustrates, this last step in the five-step process for improving customer service actually closes the cycle and serves as the springboard for its repetition. As you monitor results and collect feedback on how your service people are performing at this stage, you are actually gathering information that will lead to a refinement or redefinition of your service-quality standards as well as a restatement of your indicators of quality service. This, in turn, continues your assessment of your current situation and, of course, requires you always to be looking for ways service can be improved.

Figure 10-7

How the Five-Step Process for Improving Customer Service Becomes a Continuing Cycle

I.

Define Your Standards of Quality Service with Measurable Indicators

⇩

II.

Assess Your Current Situation

⇩

III.

Develop Effective Service-Improvement Strategies

⇩

IV.

Initiate Your Solutions Carefully

⇩

V.

Provide Feedback, Recognition, and Rewards

Refinement and Redefinition

In sum, the cycle is repeated over and over again. In this way, improving customer service becomes a never-ending process—just as it should be.

The Top of the
Crop Restaurant

Epilogue

AS A result of declining business, the Run o' the Mill restaurant closed its doors just a few months after the Pleasants' visit. A group of experienced restaurant owners decided to purchase the facility and what was left of the business. The complete package was available for a very reasonable price, since the previous owners' finances had become severely crippled as a result of the poor performance of the Run o' the Mill.

The new owners changed the name of the restaurant to the Top of the Crop and brought in their own management team to run it. Fortunately, the new owners had just finished reading this book as the deal was completed. They decided that the main problem with the Run o' the Mill had been its service. So without sacrificing the quality of the food and beverage items, the price-value relationship, or the clean and unique surroundings, the owners focused their attention on improving customer service. The new management team, determined to make the restaurant successful, decided to follow this book's five-step process for improving customer service. Since most service employees were new, they were eager to learn and to help the new owners and managers be successful. In addition, the service employees were involved in each one of the service-improvement steps.

A strong emphasis on customer-service training was initiated at the Top of the Crop. In short order, this focus of time, effort, and money paid off. Initial customer counts exceeded the most optimistic projections. The word spread quickly through the community that the Top of the Crop was a great place to eat. John and Carol Pleasant were among those people who heard the news. They decided to give it a try on one of their "evenings of escape." Let's see what their evening was like and what has made the Top of the Crop so successful.

It is close to seven o'clock when the Pleasants pull into the parking lot at the Top of the Crop. Both are ready for a relaxing evening. "Oh, look at all the cars," Carol notes. "I hope we don't have a long wait like last time."

As John and Carol walk up to the front door, they notice again the striking exterior design. "This is still a pretty place, isn't it?," Carol says.

As they enter, Carol notices that the interior also still has the same wood-and-brick theme as before. The restaurant remains visually welcoming.

At first glance, it is difficult to tell whether there is a wait. The cocktail lounge looks full. John, as before, sneaks a peek into the dining room. It also looks full, not altogether a bad sign. "But," he muses, "that's what I thought the last time I was here. I hope things are going better here now than they were the last time we came."

A youthful hostess, nicely dressed, is standing behind the front desk. She sees the Pleasants as they walk up, gives them a big smile, and says, "Welcome to the Top of the Crop. Would you like to dine with us this evening?"

John responds, "Yes. There are two of us."

"Terrific," the hostess replies. "We are, however, running about a half-hour wait. Would you mind the wait? We have a nice lounge if you are so inclined."

"That will be fine."

"May I put your name on the waiting list?"

"Sure. It's Pleasant. P-L-E-A-S-A-N-T."

"Thank you very much, Mr. Pleasant. I'll come and get you when your table is ready. The lounge is just around the corner to your left. There should be plenty of seats in there for you."

John and Carol find a pair of seats in the lounge. They are just comfortably seated, when a cocktail waitress approaches their table.

"Good evening," she says with a friendly smile. "Welcome to the Top of the Crop. We have some wonderful new drink specials, if you are interested."

Carol perks up. "Sounds good. What do you have?"

"We have a new light cocktail made with cranberry liqueur. It's absolutely wonderful. We also have a great big cocktail punch that's nice for two people to share. Both of these are unique to this restaurant. Our bartender is very creative."

"I'd like to try the cranberry drink," Carol decides.

"Oh, you'll love it!," the waitress approves with enthusiasm.

John wants his usual glass of white wine.

"Thank you. You'll like our house wine. It's from Bottle Brothers. I'll be right back," says the waitress.

After she leaves, John says, "This place is sure different from the last time, isn't it?"

"It sure is," Carol replies. "I'm having a good time already."

"It's the company," John retorts dryly.

In a few minutes, the cocktail waitress returns with their drinks. "One cranberry special and one white wine. By the way, I hope you are having dinner with us. If you are I would be glad to put this on your dinner ticket."

"That would be great," John replies.

"Now to be sure I get this ticket to the right person, I need the name you left at the front desk."

"Pleasant."

"Thank you, Mr. Pleasant. Enjoy your drinks."

John and Carol enjoy their time together in the lounge, talking about how pleased they are with the new decor in the living room. About halfway through their cocktails, the waitress stops by.

"How is that cranberry special?"

"Delicious!," Carol responds.

"I'll be back in a bit to see if you want another."

"Oh, I think this one will be just fine."

"I'm glad you like it." The waitress smiles and proceeds to another table.

In a few minutes, the hostess approaches their table and says, "Mr. Pleasant, we have your table ready now."

"Boy, that was the fastest half-hour on record," John thinks to himself.

"Here, let me carry your cocktails for you," the hostess offers, producing a small round tray designed for the job.

John and Carol smile and follow the waitress to their table. As they walk, the hostess asks them if they have been to the Top of the Crop before.

Carol answers, "No. This is the first time. But we were here when it was that other restaurant."

"The Run o' the Mill. But please don't judge us by them," the hostess says with a smile. "Here we are. Will this table be all right?"

"Just fine," John and Carol respond, in unison.

"Here are your menus and a wine list in case you are interested in some wine with your dinner. Your waiter tonight will be Frank. He should be along in just a minute. Thank you for waiting so patiently, and I hope you enjoy your meal. By the way, the scallop special is very good!"

"Why, thank you for that suggestion," Carol says.

"You're welcome. Here comes Frank now." The hostess smiles and departs.

The waiter approaches the table. "Good evening, Mr. Pleasant," he says.

John is thunderstruck that he is called by name. "This guy is off to a good start," he thinks to himself.

"My name is Frank, and I want to welcome you both to the Top of the Crop tonight," Frank says with a big smile.

"Thank you," John replies.

"Before you have a chance to look at your menu, I would like to describe a special we have this evening, and then I will give you a few minutes to think about your choice. The special tonight is a fresh salmon, broiled and served in a light butter and dill sauce. It's very good! It comes with a choice of potatoes and fresh-cooked vegetables." Frank's voice is friendly and enthusiastic as he describes the salmon special, and his eye contact makes it clear to John that he wants to make sure they understand completely what the dish is like. "May I get you anything to drink, or perhaps a nice shrimp cocktail, or one of our delicious oyster appetizers while you are deciding?"

John looks at Carol. "Oh, I think not. But we would like to order some wine with our dinner."

"I can bring out the wine now, if you wish."

"Terrific." John looks at the wine list and doesn't see anything familiar. "Hmm. It's hard to choose," he says.

"Do you prefer a white or a red wine?," Frank asks.

"I think we are up for some white wine tonight," John responds, looking at Carol for affirmation.

"Then may I suggest a bottle of Crock's Chenin Blanc? It's nice—dry and very smooth. The price is also reasonable."

"Sounds good to me," John replies with a smile.

"Fine. I'll be back in a few minutes with your wine. Take your time looking over the menu."

After Frank leaves, Carol asks John, "What are you going to have?"

"Oh, the New York strip looks good."

"I should have known. I can't make up my mind. The menu is great, isn't it?"

Frank arrives with the bottle of wine. While he opens the bottle he asks, "Do you have any questions about anything on the menu?"

Carol does. "I can't decide between the crab legs, the scallops, and the swordfish. Which one do you recommend?"

"Well, let me help by telling you a little about each one, okay?"

Carol nods.

"The crab legs are superb. You get a healthy portion of steamed Alaskan king crab legs with the shells split. They are served with a huge pot of melted butter. The scallops are the large variety, simmered in a cheese and wine sauce on a bed of long-grained rice. We are getting rave reviews from customers tonight about them. We are also very lucky to have swordfish, since it is a seasonal item. It is fresh and broiled quickly on our mesquite grill. It is about an inch thick and tastes as good as any steak."

"You make them all sound so good," Carol says with a smile.

"I don't think you could go wrong with the scallops. The chef has really outdone herself with them tonight."

"I'm sold. I'll try the scallops," Carol decides.

"And I will have the New York strip, medium rare, please," John says.

Frank nods and says, "Along with your meals, may I suggest an order of spiced steamed artichokes? It will complement your meals perfectly."

"Sounds good. Bring us one," John replies.

When the meals arrive, both John and Carol are extremely pleased with their selections. The food is, indeed, very good. About half-way through the meal, Frank stops by and inquires, "Is that steak cooked the way you like it?"

John responds, "The steak is very fine, thank you."

Frank turns to Carol. "Well, what can I tell the chef about the scallops? Are they up to your expectations?"

"Tell her they are superb—just excellent," Carol says happily.

As Frank turns to leave, he reminds them, "Now, don't forget to leave room for dessert. We've got some great ones!"

When Frank stops back to pick up the empty plates, he says, with a smile, "Now, you can't leave without trying our famous berry dessert, or at least our chocolate mousse. Either one goes great with a cup of coffee or an after-dinner drink."

John looks at Carol and Carol looks at John. "Do you want to split a mousse?," Carol asks John.

"Sure, why not? Along with two coffees—black, please."

"Coming right up," Frank responds with a smile.

When the mousse is gone and the coffee cups are almost empty, Frank comes back with the check and the coffee pot. "How about some more coffee?," he asks. "I hope everything went well for you this evening, Mr. and Mrs. Pleasant. We do hope to see you here again soon."

"I think you are going to see a lot of us here," John replies.

"I think so too," Carol agrees.

"You know," John says to Carol, as they leave, "if I owned a restaurant, I would want it run the way this one is run. They really do the job right."

Index

About the Author

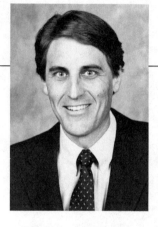

William B. Martin, formerly director of organizational development for Cask 'n' Cleaver Restaurants, is active as a consultant specializing in training and development. His clients include Holiday Inns, PepsiCo Food Service, Saga, All-American Restaurants, and In-N-Out Burger, Inc.

He is currently an associate professor of hospitality management at California State Polytechnic University, and he holds a Ph.D. in educational administration.

His past work experience includes managing professional-development programs for the military, General Dynamics, Rockwell, and Lockheed.

He is also the author of *The Fifty-Minute Restaurant Server,* published by Crisp Publications (95 First St., Los Altos, CA 94022).